Security Modeling
and Analysis of
Mobile Agent Systems

SERIES IN ELECTRICAL AND COMPUTER ENGINEERING **VOL. 5**

Security Modeling and Analysis of Mobile Agent Systems

Lu Ma

Jeffrey J. P. Tsai

University of Illinois at Chicago, USA

Imperial College Press

Published by

Imperial College Press
57 Shelton Street
Covent Garden
London WC2H 9HE

Distributed by

World Scientific Publishing Co. Pte. Ltd.
5 Toh Tuck Link, Singapore 596224
USA office: 27 Warren Street, Suite 401-402, Hackensack, NJ 07601
UK office: 57 Shelton Street, Covent Garden, London WC2H 9HE

British Library Cataloguing-in-Publication Data
A catalogue record for this book is available from the British Library.

ISBN-13 978-1-86094-634-9
ISBN-10 1-86094-634-8

Printed in Singapore

to my dear parents Bingti and Jianmin,
and my affectionate husband Zhenwei

— L. M.

to my family

— J. T.

Preface

Computer systems have evolved from early centralized computing systems into distributed computing systems. Distributed computing paradigms have also experienced a development from client-server paradigm to current mobile agent paradigm. Traditionally, *Remote Procedure Call (RPC)* is used in client-server paradigm. A client sends data to its server to invoke the execution of a remote static procedure on the server side and receives the results from the server after the computation is finished. RPC normally requires great amounts of data to be transferred across the network. Although the rapid growth of the Internet, especially the World Wide Web, provides an astounding amount of interconnected computing resources, most users' access to Internet resources are primarily restricted by the available network bandwidth. Compared to the speed of CPUs, the speed of network is still far behind. This fact stimulates seeking alternatives for moving data across a network to improve the computing efficiency.

The mobile agent paradigm is an extension to distributed computing paradigms. A mobile agent is a software program with mobility which can be sent out from a computer into a network and roam among the computer nodes in the network. Mobile agent systems are currently being developed by industry, government, and academia. The application areas include, but are not restricted to the following: telecommunications systems, personal digital assistants, information management, on-line auctions, service brokering, contract negotiation, air traffic control, parallel processing, and computer simulation. Although mobile agent technology has many notable advantages to be applied to a wide range, it also brings significant new security threats because the mobile code generated by one party will transfer to and execute in an environment controlled by another party. Several security issues arise in various areas for mobile agent computing, including authentication, authorization (or access control), intrusion detection, etc. This book introduces the basic concept and structure of mobile agent systems. We discuss various attacks and countermeasures, and present the security modeling and analysis of mobile agent systems. Our emphasis is on the formal modeling and analysis of a secure mobile agent system. Experiments were conducted to show the usability of the presented formal model. The book also studies two cases in electronic commerce and in E-auction using the model.

Lu Ma and Jeffrey J.P. Tsai

Contents

Preface   vii

1. INTRODUCTION 1

1.1 BACKGROUND...1

2. MOBILE AGENT SYSTEM 5

2.1 COMPONENTS OF A MOBILE AGENT SYSTEM 5
2.2 CHARACTERISTICS AND ADVANTAGES OF A MOBILE AGENT SYSTEM 6

3. ATTACKS AND COUNTERMEASURES OF SOFTWARE SYSTEM SECURITY..10

3.1 GENERAL SECURITY OBJECTIVES 11
3.2 TYPES OF ATTACKS..14
    3.2.1 Attacks against availability...14
    3.2.2 Attacks against confidentiality 15
    3.2.3 Attacks against integrity 17
    3.2.4 Attacks against miscellaneous security objectives 18
3.3 COUNTERMEASURES OF ATTACKS 19
    3.3.1 Authentication 19
    3.3.2 Access control 21
    3.3.3 Audit and intrusion detection 26
    3.3.4 Cryptography...28
    3.3.5 Firewall...32
    3.3.6 Anti-virus software..34

4. SECURITY ISSUES IN A MOBILE AGENT SYSTEM 37

4.1 SECURITY ISSUES IN A MOBILE AGENT SYSTEM 37
    4.1.1 Possible attacks to a mobile agent system 37
        4.1.1.1 Possible attacks to a mobile agent 37
        4.1.1.2 Possible attacks to a mobile agent platform.............40
    4.1.2 Security requirements for a secure mobile agent system 41
4.2 RELATED WORKS...44

4.2.1 Existing mobile agent systems 44
4.2.2 Security research 51
        4.2.2.1 Security measures for a mobile agent platform....................53
        4.2.2.2 Security measures for a mobile agent 56
4.2.3 Mobility modeling...59
4.2.4 Conclusions 61

5 A NEW FORMAL MODEL —— EXTENDED ELEMENTARY OBJECT SYSTEM (EEOS)..63

5.1 OBJECT-ORIENTED TECHNOLOGY AND PETRI NETS.............................64
5.2 ELEMENTARY OBJECT SYSTEM (EOS).................................65
5.3 EXTENDED ELEMENTARY OBJECT SYSTEM (EEOS) 68
        5.3.1 Requirements of a formal method for mobile agent system modeling..68
        5.3.2 Extensions to Elementary Object System 70
                5.3.2.1 Multiple system nets...............................70
                5.3.2.2 Multiple layers...................................70
                5.3.2.3 Token pool......................................71
                5.3.2.4 Internal places, external places and internal transitions, external transitions 72
                5.3.2.5 Two new arcs.....................................74
                5.3.2.6 Extended interaction relation.....................77
        5.3.3 Formal specification of Extended Elementary Object System ..78

6 A FORMAL FRAMEWORK OF A GENERIC SECURE MOBILE AGENT SYSTEM BASED ON EEOS..80

6.1 STRUCTURE OF A MOBILE AGENT SYSTEM 80
        6.1.1 Mobile agent platform 82
                6.1.1.1 Functionalities and components of a mobile agent platform ..83
                6.1.1.2 EEOS model of a mobile agent platform 84
        6.1.2 Trust server...92
        6.1.3 Mobile agent...98
                6.1.3.1 Functionalities and components of a mobile agent...............98
                6.1.3.2 EEOS model 99
6.2 COMMUNICATION IN A MOBILE AGENT SYSTEM..........................104
        6.2.1 Dynamic connection.....................................104
        6.2.2 Communications for a mobile agent platform and a mobile agent 107
                6.2.2.1 Communication contents 107
                6.2.2.2 Synchronous and asynchronous communications.................109
6.3 MOBILITY IN A MOBILE AGENT SYSTEM..............................113
        6.3.1 Strong mobility...113
        6.3.2 Weak mobility 118
        6.3.3 Discussion about weak mobility and strong mobility.............119

6.4 SECURITY IN A MOBILE AGENT SYSTEM..............................121
   6.4.1 Secure mobile agent transfer 122
      6.4.1.1 Formalization of the secure mobile agent transfer.............125
   6.4.2 Mutual authentication between a mobile agent and a mobile agent platform..128
   6.4.3 Authorization for a mobile agent from a mobile agent platform 131
      6.4.3.1 Authorization expression method 131
      6.4.3.2 Authorization policy....................................134
      6.4.3.3 Authorization maintenance.............................138
   6.4.4 Data security and action security..............................139
      6.4.4.1 Data security...140
      6.4.4.2 Action security...141

7 TRANSLATING THE EEOS MODEL TO COLORED PETRI NET MODEL..146

   7.1 OBJECT NET TOKENS AND SPECIAL TOKENS 147
      7.1.1 Object net tokens 147
      7.1.2 Special tokens...149
   7.2 DYNAMIC CONNECTION 150
   7.3 NEW CONSTRUCTS – TWO NEW ARCS AND EXTENDED INTERACTION RELATION 152
      7.3.1 Two new arcs..152
      7.3.2 Extended interaction relation............................152
   7.4 COMPLICATED COMMUNICATION 153

8 SIMULATION AND ANALYSIS OF THE EXTENDED ELEMENTARY OBJECT SYSTEM MODEL OF A SECURE MOBILE AGENT SYSTEM...155

   8.1 REACHABILITY...159
   8.2 BOUNDEDNESS...159
   8.3 LIVENESS 161
   8.4 CONCURRENCY 161
   8.5 SECURITY..162

9 A CASE STUDY IN ELECTRONIC COMMERCE..................166

   9.1 CASE SCENARIO..166
   9.2 EEOS MODEL 166
   9.3 SYNCHRONOUS FIRING MECHANISM IN THE CASE STUDY 168
   9.4 DESIGN/CPN MODEL AND EXPERIMENT RESULTS.................170

10 A CASE STUDY IN E-AUCTION SYSTEM........................174

   10.1 CASE SCENARIO..174
      10.1.1 ABEAS - agent based e-auctioning system...............174

10.1.1.1 The agents in ABEAS 176
10.1.1.2 The agent platform in ABEAS 176
10.1.1.3 Security issues in the ABEAS 177
10.1.2 Modeling requirements of ABEAS 177
10.2 EEOS MODEL 178
10.2.1 The e-broker agent 178
10.2.2 The modified trust server 179

11 CONCLUSION 181

BIBLIOGRAPHY 183

INDEX 199

Chapter 1

Introduction

1.1 Background

Computer systems have evolved from early centralized computing systems into distributed computing systems. Distributed computing paradigms have also experienced a development from client-server paradigm to current mobile agent paradigm. Traditionally, *Remote Procedure Call (RPC)* is used in client-server paradigm. A client sends data to its server to invoke the execution of a remote static procedure on the server side and receives the results from the server after the computation is finished. RPC normally requires great amounts of data to be transferred across the network. Although the rapid growth of the Internet, especially the World Wide Web, provides an astounding amount of interconnected computing resources, most users' access to Internet resources are primarily restricted by the available network bandwidth. Compared to the speed of CPUs, the speed of network is still far behind. This fact stimulates seeking alternatives for moving data across a network to improve the computing efficiency.

The *remote evaluation (REV)* paradigm extended the client-server concept of distributed applications by transporting program code from the local client computer to the remote server computer for execution there. REV paradigm provided a new degree of flexibility in the design of distributed systems. In distributed systems using RPC, server computers are designed to offer a fixed set of services. On the contrary, in distributed systems using REV, server computers are more properly viewed as programmable processors. Because applications are usually more compact than the data they operate upon or produce [103], REV paradigm can reduce a great amount of communication that is required to accomplish a given task.

The *code on demand (CoD)* paradigm further extended the aforementioned concept, by transferring the application logic in the reverse direction (i.e. from the remote to the local computer) and providing the computational platform and resources locally to ascertain some result. The main form of application logic in CoD paradigm is "applet". An applet is usually downloaded from a host computer as a server to a local computer as a client by using a web browser and gets executed on the local computer. The mobility of code for an applet is unidirectional and often occurs only once for one execution, although the same applet can be downloaded many times by the same computer or different computers at different times.

The *mobile agent (MA)* paradigm is a further extension to distributed computing paradigms. A mobile agent is a software program with mobility which can be sent out from a computer into a network and roam among the computer nodes in the network. It can be executed on those computers to finish its task on behalf of its owner. The direction of a mobile agent can be multi-way, from any computer to another within that network. The migration of a mobile agent can occur multiple times before it comes back to its home computer with the computation results. In addition, not only the application logic of a mobile agent is transferred between computers, but the application state can be transferred from one computer to another. The transferring of a mobile agent state facilitates it in working autonomously to travel between one or more remote computers. Figure 1 illustrates the distributed computing paradigms introduced above.

The use of mobile code has a long history dating back to the use of remote job entry systems in the 1960's. Today's mobile agent incarnations can be characterized in a number of ways ranging from simple distributed objects to highly organized software with embedded intelligence [64]. Mobile agent paradigm helps form a large-scale, loosely-coupled distributed system. Because of its many salient merits, it has attracted tremendous attention in the last few years and become a promising direction in distributed computing and processing, as well as high performance network area.

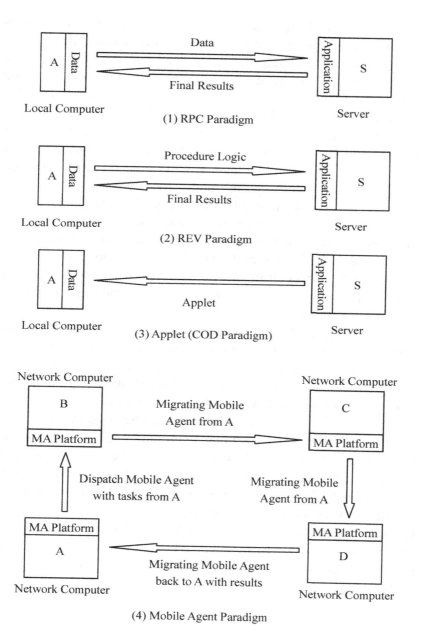

Figure 1 Evolution of Distributed Computing Paradigms

Although mobile agent technology has many notable advantages to be applied to a wide range, it also brings significant new security threats because the mobile code generated by one party will transfer to and execute in an environment controlled by another party. Several security issues arise in various areas for mobile agent computing, including authentication, authorization (or access control), intrusion detection, etc. A mobile agent system could be attacked by malicious agents, platforms and third parties. Many of these threats have counterparts in conventional client-server systems and have always existed in some form in the past. Mobile agents simply offer a greater opportunity for abuse and misuse, which broadens the scale of threats significantly. In addition, since mobile agents have some unique characteristics such as the mobility of a mobile agent, security problems become more complicated in mobile agent systems. Those security problems have become the bottleneck of the development and maintenance of mobile agent technology, especially in security sensitive applications such as electronic commerce.

A lot of research has been dedicated to address the security problems in a mobile agent system. This research differs in its aim, emphasis, base, and technique. Some work are towards building the foundations for the security of a mobile agent system; some propose security mechanisms following different approaches; some focus on introducing security mechanisms into the architectures of mobile code systems; and others implement real applications with security features. However, there has been limited research dedicated to provide an intuitive formal framework for a secure mobile agent system, including formal modeling of mobility, communication, and execution. This book introduces the concept and structure of mobile agent systems, discusses various attacks and countermeasures, and presents the security modeling and analysis of mobile agent systems. Our emphasis is on the formal modeling and analysis of a secure mobile agent system and its applications.

Chapter 2

Mobile Agent System

2.1 Components of a Mobile Agent System

A mobile agent system consists of two main components: mobile agents and their platforms (or hosts). Mobile agents are software agents which are goal-directed and can automatically suspend their execution on one platform and migrate to another platform, where they resume execution to accomplish their tasks, within a network they can travel around. Gray et al [53] succinctly define a mobile agent as follows:

*A **mobile agent** is an executing program that can migrate, at times of its own choosing, from machine to machine in a heterogeneous network. On each machine, the agent interacts with stationary service agents and other resources to accomplish its task.*

Kalchuk and Karmouch further extend the definition in [112] by stipulating that:

The agent decides when and where it will migrate, and may interrupt its own execution and continue elsewhere on the network.

A mobile agent consists of code and its current configuration, including global data structures, stacks, heap, and control information such as the program counter. Generally speaking, a mobile agent has its code (static), data, and state. Its state composes of two parts. One is "data state", which records the values of all the global and local variables. The other is "execution state", which records the states of all processes and threads. An agent's data and state would change dynamically due to its execution and migration. There are two kinds of agent mobility: weak mobility and strong mobility. The former only includes the migration of code and data, while the latter includes the migration of code, data and state. If strong migration is considered, all of these three components of a mobile agent may be tampered with in an insecure environment. A mobile agent should be able to communicate with other agents, and can continue to operate even after its home platform, the platform which launches it, has been removed from the network. Therefore, it offers great advantages in reducing the network traffic as well as increasing the network efficiency.

Mobile agent platforms are the executing environments for mobile agents on different computers, including the home platforms and guest platforms. A home platform of a mobile agent is responsible for creating, initializing, dispatching, receiving, and eliminating a mobile agent. But it cannot monitor where the mobile agent travels and how it performs its tasks. The home platform environment is the most secure environment for that mobile agent. Once a mobile agent leaves this environment and travels to other mobile agent platforms, it might be attacked during the journey by some malicious subjects. A guest platform is on a machine which a mobile agent migrates to and continues its execution on. The guest platform environment provides necessary resources and information for the mobile agent. A mobile agent might communicate and exchange data with the platform directly, or with other agents on that guest platform via the platform, and obtain what it desires finally. If its entire task has not been accomplished yet after accessing a guest platform, it might jump to other guest platforms in succession. In the end, it returns to its home platform.

Besides mobile agents and mobile agent platforms, a mobile agent system may have some third parties, for example, static agents residing on mobile agent platforms or other programs which may communicate with mobile agent platforms.

2.2 Characteristics and Advantages of a Mobile Agent System

A mobile agent system has several characteristics which distinguish it from other distributed computing systems. A mobile agent is an active object — that is, objects that move from place to place and, when it arrives at a place, can obtain a thread of control automatically; it interacts with various environments to find out information or perform actions on those machines; it is capable in obtaining information or performing actions on behalf of the person who sent the agent out on the network; it has the ability to report its work's results to the requesting person after doing its work; and it can make decisions on behalf of the person it represents.

Mobile agent technology provides various advantages which make it a promising area. Although there are alternate methods of achieving the same or similar goals and functionalities of a mobile agent system, a combination of individual advantages of mobile agent technology represents an overwhelming motivation for the adoption of mobile agent systems [26]. We are highlighting several prominent strengths of mobile agent technology in the following [53][128].

First of all, bandwidth can be conserved and saved in a network using mobile agent technology. A mobile agent can perform its execution locally on some guest platform, do data filtering and only return the final result or desired data back to its home platform. No operation and communication between guest and home platforms are needed during the execution of the mobile agent. Therefore, the total completion time and communication cost could be reduced too. This feature also benefits those problems with highly interactive requirements while a mobile agent can hold a long conversation with the host on behalf of its home platform. Better scalability can be provided as a result.

Second, mobile computing and mobile clients are better supported. Typically, mobile devices such as a laptop computer are only connected to a network intermittently. Therefore, they have access to a server intermittently. Sometimes, even when connected, they have low bandwidth connection. They may have limited storage and processing capacity, too. With mobile agent, these factors won't become obstacles to use mobile computer. A mobile agent, once it is dispatched by its mobile agent platform, can travel and get executed elsewhere independently from the platform, and it helps with reducing the network traffic.

Third, dynamic load balancing can be achieved. If the workload can be distributed equitably among the whole system, the performance can be improved. While static load balancing is only based on the work allocated before execution begins, it cannot adapt to the change of work load in the real world. Mobile agents supported dynamic load balancing, because they can move across homogeneous and heterogeneous platforms carrying all application code with them, rather than pre-install that code on the destination platforms.

Fourth, dynamic deployment is facilitated. With dynamic deployment, certain software component can be installed and invoked dynamically on some remote machine by an application, as if it were pre-installed on that machine as part of the available service. Concerning mobile agent technology, a mobile agent just installs and invokes itself when it moves to a remote platform and resumes its execution there. This feature allows for more scalable applications.

Fifth, asynchronous tasks can be accomplished more effectively. A mobile agent can carry the entire task to the network and finish it asynchronously with respect to its home platform, rather than a single asynchronous process or communication.

Sixth, mobile-agent-based communications can be more robust and cheap when compared to the traditional RPC-based (Remote Procedure Call) applications because a mobile agent is executing directly on the mobile agent platform that it is communicating with. No worry is needed about packet recovery and varying rate of service over a network. This communication is reliable without added header and error correcting protocols that exist in client-server networks, thus the overhead in message processing is reduced. This communication is cheap because it eliminates the requirement that every message in a secure RPC conversation must be encrypted or signed because a mobile agent is only encrypted and authenticated once per host.

Some other advantages are also provided by mobile agent technology, such as facilitating software distribution on demand, more flexible expression of transitions, providing semantic routing, etc. More details about the advantages that a mobile agent system can bring can be found in [26] [52]etc.

A mobile agent can combine knowledge and data from its home platform and platforms it migrates to, and perform inference on the hosting platforms where the data and computing resources are located. It supports robust computing over unreliable public networks. It can provide better support for mobile computers that are only intermittently connected to a network and hence intermittently accessed to a server; and mobile computers that have low bandwidth connection when connected to a network and have limited storage and processing capacity. It facilitates real-time interaction with a server. It also enables users to create customized communicating applications by creating and deploying agents that reside at remote servers. Chess et. al. explores and analyzes the advantages of mobile agent technology in detail in [26]. Mobile agent systems are currently being developed by industry, government, and academia. The application areas include, but are not restricted to the following: telecommunications systems, personal digital assistants, information management, on-line auctions, service brokering, contract negotiation, air traffic control, parallel processing, and computer simulation.

Chapter 3

Attacks and Countermeasures of Software System Security

With rapid growth of networking, in particular the Internet, a large variety of information could be accessed by different users all over the world through a number of software systems. However, the development of corresponding security mechanisms does not parallel with the development of the networks and software systems. Many attacks occur and cause big losses. According to ZDNet Security News dated January 2004, "Computer virus attacks cost global businesses an estimated $55 billion in damages in 2003, a sum that is expected to increase this year." And virus is only one kind of attacks. Therefore, security has become a major concern of today's software systems, especially distributed systems. Software security consists of lots of aspects, such as cryptography, access control and trust management, intrusion detection and tamper resistance, authentication and privacy, signature schemes, E-commerce, security analysis, mobile computing security, and etc. An amount of research works has been devoted to those areas and different methods have been proposed.

In order to design and develop security mechanisms to protect software systems, different kinds of attacks and countermeasures against those attacks should be identified. In this chapter, we provide an overview of general categories of attacks and countermeasures existing in software system security. We then emphasize on the security problems in mobile agent system, an active and promising direction in mobile computing and distributed processing, and briefly present our formal model for mobile agent system security.

3.1 General Security Objectives

It is helpful to identify security objectives before discussing various security problems in software systems. Different systems and applications have their own security objectives; while they share quite a few common ones. Generally speaking, a secure software system should meet the following security objectives, some of which are explained based on NIST definitions [142][143]in alphabetical order below.

1. Accountability

   Accountability is the security goal that generates the requirement for actions of an entity to be traced uniquely to that entity. This objective requires that users and administrators will be held accountable for behavior that impacts the security of information. Accountability is often an organizational policy requirement and directly supports non-repudiation, deterrence, fault isolation, intrusion detection and prevention, and after-action recovery and legal action. This objective has more importance in electronic business. For example, a customer intends to buy a certain product from an online store. The user and the store have a session of communications, so that the user tells the store about his credit card to be charged, and the store gives the user a receipt. Both the user and the store should be accountable for their communications and behaviors.

2. Assurance

   Assurance grounds for confidence that other security goals (including integrity, availability, confidentiality, and accountability) have been adequately met by a specific implementation. "Adequately met" includes (1) functionality that performs correctly, (2) sufficient protection against unintentional errors (by users or software), and (3) sufficient resistance to intentional penetration or by-pass.

3. Authentication

   Authentication requires verifying the identity of a user, process, or device, often as a prerequisite to allowing access to resources in a system. This objective requires that the identity (or other relevant information) of an entity or the originator of data can be verified and assured. Satisfying this objective can prevent faking or masquerading from happening

4. Authorization

Authorization is to grant or deny access rights to a user, program or process. This objective requires that only legitimate users can have the rights to use certain services or to access certain resources, while unauthorized users are kept out. It is also called "access control". Authorization is often combined with authentication as the result of authentication is usually used to decide whether or not to grant a request of an entity. To achieve those security properties, digital signatures may be required in addition to password access.

5. Availability

Availability is the security goal that generates the requirement for protection against intentional or accidental attempts to perform unauthorized deletion of data, or cause unavailability of service. This objective requires that data and system can be accessed by legitimate users within an appropriate period of time. Some attacks such as Denial of Service or instability of the system may cause loss of availability.

6. Confidentiality

Confidentiality is the security goal that generates the requirement for protection from intentional or accidental attempts to perform unauthorized data reads. Confidentiality covers data in storage, during processing, and while in transit. This objective requires that data should be protected from any unauthorized disclosure. That is to say, it should be ensured that data can only be read by persons or machines for which it is intended. A loss of confidentiality hurts the data privacy.

7. Integrity

Integrity can be classified into data integrity and system integrity. Data integrity is the objective that data should not be altered or destroyed in an unauthorized manner to maintain consistency. It also covers data in storage, during processing, and while in transit. System integrity is the objective that a system should be free from unauthorized manipulation when it performs its intended function in an unimpaired manner.

8. Non-repudiation

This objective requires that either side of a communication cannot deny the communication later. Important communication exchanges must be logged to prevent later denials by any party of a transaction. This objective also relies on authentication to record the identities of entities.

Besides the objectives mentioned above, more security objectives may be identified and required in different situations. Generally speaking, accountability, availability, assurance, confidentiality and integrity are five main security objectives of a software system. These security objectives are not isolated. Instead, various relationships exist among them. Assurance is the base security objective that other objectives are built on. Confidentiality and integrity can affect and also be affected by each other. Based on them, availability and accountability can be achieved.

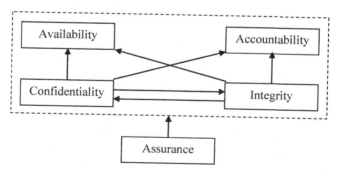

Figure 2 Relationship among Five Main Security Objectives

Figure 2 shows the relationships among these five main security objectives. For a specific system, certain security objectives may conflict to each other sometimes. For example, to increase the availability level, a system may have to compromise its confidentiality or integrity level. Therefore, an overall security policy is often preferred other than individual security objectives.

3.2 Types of Attacks

It is desired that a software system can meet all security objectives. But many issues compromise the system security. The most severe issue is various attacks which take advantage of the weakness and vulnerability of a system, and try to breach the system. A lot of attacks have been noticed and tackled with, while more new attacks are hiding or arising. It is helpful to know how many types of attacks are there and what their characteristics are. Viewed from different aspects, attacks to a software system can be classified into different categories. In this chapter, we summarize and categorize types of attacks based on their negative effects on security objectives. Therefore, most existing attacks fall into three major categories: attacks against availability, attacks against confidentiality, and attacks against integrity. It should be note that these categories may be overlapping since quite a few attacks have multiple targets. Since this chapter is more from the technique point of view, certain attacks and threats which involve personal factors, such as social engineering threats, are ignored here.

3.2.1 *Attacks against availability*

Attacks against availability mainly attempt to overload available resources or make a particular facility unavailable at a certain time for the attackers' sake. Sometimes, such attacks may not totally disable targeted resources and services, but just degrade them. Attacks in this category are usually DoS (Denial of Service) attacks.

According to CERT® Coordination Center [23], a DoS attack is characterized by an explicit attempt by attackers to prevent legitimate users from using system services, or cause delaying of time-critical operations. Time-critical may be milliseconds or hours, depending upon the service provided. Typically, DoS attacks can result in the unavailability of a particular network service or the temporary loss of all network connectivity and services. They can also destroy programming and files in a computer system. A commonly seen DoS attack on the Internet is simply to send more traffic to a network node than it is supposed to take, such that the functionality of that network node gets disabled. An example of such DoS attack is the smurf attack or a PING flood, in which a smurf attacker sends PING requests to an Internet broadcast address and spoofs the return address as the target victim's address. The victim's network line would be filled by these PING replies and its network service would be brought to its knees. SYN flood attack is another example of DoS attack using the similar strategy to PING flood.

DoS attacks come in a variety of forms and aim at a variety of services. Following are three basic modes of attacks:

(1) Consumption of scarce, limited, or non-renewable resources;
(2) Destruction or alteration of configuration information;
(3) Physical destruction or alteration of network components.

DoS attacks usually occur intentionally and maliciously, but they can also happen accidentally. Dos attacks usually do not result in the theft of information or other security loss. However, these attacks can cost the target system significant time and money.

3.2.2 *Attacks against confidentiality*

Attacks against confidentiality mainly attempt to reveal the contents of communications, or leak sensitive data and information of a system. Attacks in this category have different forms, while the Eavesdrop attack is a primary class.

An Eavesdrop attack is an attack where communication is monitored to reveal the secret. It usually occurs when some wiretap devices are plugged into computer networks and eavesdrop on the network traffic. Then a sniffing program lets someone listen to computer conversations. However, computer conversations consist of apparently random binary data. Therefore, network wiretap programs also come with a feature known as "protocol analysis", which allow them to decode the computer traffic and make sense of it.

Originally, the base for this type of attack is the shared principle on which the Ethernet is built, which is, all machines on a local network share the same wire. Therefore, all machines are able to "see" all the traffic on the same wire. Ethernet hardware is built with a filter that ignores all traffic that does not belong to it. A wiretap program turns off this filter, and put the Ethernet hardware into promiscuous mode. Later networks are developed from share mode to switch mode. Electronic eavesdropping, which applies electromagnetic devices such as a frequency analyzer and a tuned antenna, emerges as well. They are often taken advantage of by amateur eavesdroppers to perform eavesdrop attack. Eavesdrop attacks usually cost the loss of confidentiality and secrecy of a system, but do not hurt integrity.

Another form of attacks against confidentiality is data aggregation, which allows an attacker to deduce classified information from unclassified information. For example, an attacker may determine a specific employee's approximate salary by looking into the department's personnel expenditure before and after hiring this employee.

Password or encryption key sniffing also do harm to system confidentiality. This kind of attack enable an attacker gain unauthorized access to system or facilities by stealing legitimate users' passwords and masquerading as the legitimate user, or inspect encrypted files or communication messages by using encryption keys got illegally. This attack usually takes advantage of the "broadcast" technology used in most networks. When a legitimate user tries to log into a system remotely, or an entity of a communication tries to request an encryption key, the attacker's computer can get those secure information if the security of the network is not strong enough. It should be note that after a password or encryption key has been sniffed by an attacker, he/she can go ahead to perform certain attacks to hurt system integrity.

3.2.3 *Attacks against integrity*

Attacks against integrity mainly attempt to modify communication contents or data in a system. Attacks in this category also have many various forms.

One primary form is the Man-In-The-Middle (MITM) attack, which happens when an attacker sniffs packets from network, modifies them and inserts them back into the network. In MITM attack, an attacker is able to read and modify messages between two parties at his/her will, without letting either entity know that they have been attacked. MITM attacks remain a primary weakness of public-key based system. The introduction of signed keys by a trusted third party can help with designing a mechanism for coping with such attacks.

Another form is the Web Site Defacing and Hijacking attack. This type of attack may modify, destroy or replace some web pages of certain institutions. Visitors of those institutions are given altered information, or hijacked to other site without knowing the fact. Attackers can then request and collect certain information or gain benefits from the clients. Weaknesses of web server are always the base for this type of attacks.

Attacks on authentication usually hurt integrity as well. Such attacks generally allow an attacker to masquerade as a user with higher privilege then him/her. As we introduced in section 3.2, password sniffing is used towards password-based authentication systems to perform attacks against confidentiality and integrity, while disclosure of encryption key is used towards cryptographic authentication systems. For the latter system, replay attack exists as well. A replay attack is an attack in which the attacker records data or communication contents and replays it later to deceive the recipient. For example, the initiator of a session Alice sends and receives several messages to and from the responder of this session Bob, while an intruder Elisa stores all the messages. After this session is over, Elisa may send the packages sent by Alice before to Bob again in order to impersonate as Alice in a new session. If Elisa succeeds, Bob is tricked to believe he has another session with Alice. Therefore Elisa can use Alice's privilege to access and modify information or resources of Bob.

3.2.4 *Attacks against miscellaneous security objectives*

Attacks are not always towards one single security objective. On the contrary, many of them have multiple security objectives as their attacking targets. Viruses, unauthorized access attacks, and code exploit attacks are to be introduced below as three examples in this category.

Viruses are self propagating entities that move across the nodes of the Internet. The life cycle of a virus begins when it is created and ends when it is completely eradicated. Its complete life cycle contains the following stages: creation, replication, activation, discovery, assimilation, and eradication. It is not hard to understand the creation, replication and eradication. So we will only explain the rest three stages in more details here. A virus with damage routine will be activated when certain conditions are met, for example, on a certain day or when the infected user performs a particular action. On the contrary, a virus without damage routine does not activate. Instead, they only cause damage by stealing storage space. The "discovery" stage usually follows activation, but not necessarily. When a virus is discovered, it is sent to certain organizations for documenting and to those antivirus software developers for analysis. Then antivirus software developers modify their software so that the software can detect or kill the new virus. This stage is called "assimilation". The ability to replicate is the unique characteristic of viruses. Another commonality is that they may contain a damage routine that delivers the virus payload towards system confidentiality and system integrity. Such payload may destroy files, reformat hard drive, or cause other damages. Even if a virus does not contain a damage routine, it can still degrade the overall performance of a system to its legitimate users by consuming storage space and memory, which hurt system availability.

Unauthorized access attacks include unauthorized use of resources and illicit access of data. An attacker may impersonate as a legal user or bypass the authorization procedure which is not designed very well. The "backdoor" may be used to perform such attack. A backdoor in a computer system is a method of bypassing normal authentication or obtaining remote access to a computer, while intended to remain hidden to inspection. The backdoor may take the form of an installed program or could be a modification to a legitimate program. This type of attack may hurt system and user confidentiality as well as their integrity.

No software system is perfect. Code exploit attacks exploit software flaws to gain control of a computer, or to cause it to operate in an unexpected manner. Such attacks often come in the form of Trojan horses, for example, non-executable media files which are disguised to function in the system. Code quality is a key point when code exploit attack is taken into consideration. Some development methodologies rely on testing to ensure the quality of any code released. But they often fail to discover extremely unusual potential exploits. According to the difference of software flaws being exploited, this kind of attack may do harm to system confidentiality, integrity and availability.

3.3 Countermeasures of Attacks

In order to counter various attacks, a lot of methods have been designed and proposed. Although they cannot solve all problems, they increase the security level of a software system. A countermeasure does not necessarily aim at one single attack. On the contrary, many countermeasures can provide protection against multiple attacks. These countermeasures may be applied in different layers of a computer system, such as physical layer or network layer, operating system layer which includes file system management, database management layer, or application layer. In the following, we introduce some categories of countermeasures. They are high-level techniques, and there are various concrete techniques to implement them.

3.3.1 *Authentication*

When considered as a countermeasure of attacks, authentication refers to the process whereby one entity proves its identity to another entity. In many situations, authentication is the most primary security service on which other security services depend. Ensuring authentication plays an important role in reinforcing those security objectives of a software system, such as accountability, authorization, confidentiality, integrity, and non-repudiation. Authentication is also a powerful shield protecting a software system from attacks towards those security objectives. In most cases, authentication establishes the identity of a human user to a computer system and is called "user-computer authentication". In other cases, authentication is also needed between computers or processes in a distributed environment. These two types of authentication are to be introduced below [130].

(1) User-Computer Authentication

User-computer authentication is often done through checking of passwords, cryptographic token or smart card, or biometric features such as a fingerprint. Password-based authentication is the most common technique and has been widely used. But it is vulnerable to attacks since a password can be guessed and shared. It is desired that a user can choose his/her passwords intelligently and change the passwords regularly. Authentication using a cryptographic token or smart card is much stronger than using passwords, because the token or a smart card is a hardware device equipped with a cryptographic key. This key does not leave the hardware device. But the token or smart card can also be shared or stolen. Biometric authentication takes advantage of the fact that biometric features are different from person to person. It has been used for applications requiring high level security. But it is also vulnerable to replay attacks and it needs cumbersome equipments. Therefore, combination of these methods is really needed.

(2) Authentication in Distributed Systems

In a distributed system, authentication is required repeatedly when a user accesses multiple machines and uses multiple services. Typically a user logs into a workstation using his/her password and then the workstation connects to other computers in this system on the user's behalf. Authentication becomes more complicated in a distributed system. One reason is that some third party can fake as others by actively eavesdropping or wiretapping others' communications. Drawbacks in some communication protocols are also used by attackers to achieve this goal. Therefore formal methods should be used to verify the correctness of those protocols before they are put into use [94].

Authentication is usually implemented using two methods, one of which is called "message authentication code", the other is called "digital signature". A message authentication code is a short and non-transferable signature on a document. It is specific to an entity and cannot be verified by other entities. So it cannot be transferred and therefore cannot be used for contracts or receipts, which need to be saved and verified in case of a conflict. But it can be used for entities to make sure that the message they obtain is from the entity they expect. A message authentication code requires that the sender and the receiver of the authenticated message both know a symmetric secret used to generate and verify the message authentication code. This secret can be produced by one of the participants, and sent over in an encrypted form to the other, using a public key encryption method. Message authentication codes can be implemented using stream ciphers, e.g., RC5. Since a message authentication code is very efficient, it is useful for individual, small messages in interactive protocols. A digital signature is an authentication on a document and is computed using the secret key or private key of the signer on the document. A signature can be verified by anyone using the public key of the signer, the document signed, and the signature on the document. Therefore it can be transferred and useful for contracts, receipts, etc. A digital signature is usually long, e.g. 1024 bits, and not very quick to produce and verify. For these reasons, digital signatures should only be used when message authentication codes cannot offer the required functionalities.

3.3.2 *Access control*

Access control is the collection of mechanisms that permits managers of a system to exercise a directing or restraining influence over the behaviors, usage and contents of a system. It permits management to specify what users can do, which resources they can access and what operations they can perform. This technique is also known as "authorization". It is quite essential in software system security, as it grounds for higher-level security objectives such as confidentiality and integrity. Appropriate access control may prevent a software system from certain attacks, such as unauthorized access attacks.

Since access control is the process of determining whether an identity (plus a set of attributes associated with that identity) is permitted to perform some action like accessing a resource; access control usually requires authentication as a prerequisite. Authentication and access control decisions can be made at different points by different organizations. But these two are not necessarily separated. A number of security products or protocols implement these two procedures together, such as the IEEE 802.1x. It is an open-standards-based protocol for authenticating network clients or ports on a user ID basis. It takes the RADIUS methodology and separates it into three distinct groups: the Supplicant, the Authenticator and the Authentication Server. This protocol provides a means of restricting network access to authorized users.

It is necessary to make a distinction between access control policies and access control mechanisms. Policies are high level guidelines which determine how accesses are controlled and how access decisions are determined. Mechanisms are low level software and hardware functions which can be configured to implement a policy. Generally speaking, there are three access control policies [134].

(1) Mandatory Access Control

Mandatory access control (MAC) policy compares the sensitivity label at which the user is working to the sensitivity label of the object being accessed. If MAC checks are passed, the user is given the access rights on the object. If not, the access request will be refused. MAC is mandatory because the labeling of information happens automatically, and ordinary users cannot change labels unless they are authorized by an administrator.

When the security policy of a system has the following two requirements: (1) the protection decisions must not be decided by the object owner; and (2) the system must enforce the protection decisions, the need for a mandatory access control (MAC) mechanism arises. MAC policy is supported by POSIX.6 standard, which provides a labeling mechanism and a set of interfaces that can be used to determine access based on the MAC policy.

(2) Discretionary Access Control

Discretionary access control (DAC) is the most common type of access control policy implemented in computer systems today. It restricts access to objects based on the identity of users and/or groups to which they belong. DAC is discretionary since a user with certain access permission is capable of passing that permission to any other user directly or indirectly. DAC controls are used to restrict a user's access to protected objects on the system. The user may also be restricted to a subset of the possible access rights available for those protected objects. Access rights are the operations a user may perform on a particular objects, e.g., read, write, execute. Since DAC restricts access to objects based solely on the identity of users who are trying to access them, the identities of both the users and objects are the key to DAC. In most systems, any program which runs on behalf of a user inherits the DAC access rights of that user. This basic principle of DAC contains a fundamental flaw that makes it vulnerable to Trojan horses.

Since the DAC permissions on system objects, usually files, can only be changed by the administrator who owns them, DAC is often used along with MAC to control access to system files.

(3) Role-based Access Control

Role-based access control (RBAC) is receiving increasing attention as a generalized approach to access control. In a RBAC model, roles represent functions granted within a given organization and authorizations. Authorizations granted to a role are strictly related to the data objects and resources that are needed by a user in order to exercise the functions of the role. Users are thus simply authorized to "play" the appropriate roles, by acquiring the roles' authorizations. When a user logs in a system using RBAC, s/he can activate a subset of the roles s/he is authorized to play. The use of roles has several well recognized advantages. Because roles represent organizational functions, a role-based model can directly support security policies of the organization. Authorization administration is also greatly simplified. If a user moves to a new function within the organization, there is no need to revoke the authorizations s/he had in the previous function and then grant the authorizations he/she needs in the new function. The security administrator simply needs to revoke and grant the appropriate role membership. RBAC models have also been shown to be able to support multiple access control policies. In particular, by appropriately configuring a role system, a RBAC model can support MAC and DAC as well.

Different mechanisms are used to implement the access control policies introduced above, such as Access Control Lists (ACLs), capabilities, and authorization table, which are different methods to store the access matrix of a system [13]. An access matrix is a spreadsheet with columns as resources, rows as users, and items as access rights the user in the corresponding row has over the object in the corresponding column. It is the simplest framework for describing a protection system.

(1) Access Control Lists (ACLs)

ACLs correspond to storing the access matrix by columns. They are associated with system objects and contain entries specifying the access that individual users or groups of users have to these objects. Access control lists provide a straightforward way of granting or denying access for a specified user or groups of users to a particular object. An access control list is a table that tells a computer operating system which access rights users have over a particular system object, such as a file directory or an individual file. Each object has a security attribute that identifies its access control list. The list has an entry for each system user with access privileges. The most common privileges for a file include the ability to read, write, and execute if the file is executable. Microsoft Windows NT/2000, Novell's NetWare, Digital's OpenVMS, and Unix-based systems are among the operating systems that use access control lists. The list is implemented differently by each operating system.

(2) Capabilities

Capabilities correspond to storing the access matrix by rows. Therefore they are associated with system users and contain entries specifying the access rights each individual user or each group of users has to the system objects. Capabilities provide a straightforward way of identifying what objects can be accessed by a user or a group and how they can be accessed. Capabilities encapsulate object identity. When a process presents a capability on behalf of a user, the operating system examines the capability to determine both the object and the corresponding access. The location of the object in memory is encapsulated in the capability.

Similarly to ACLs, capabilities also aim at directly providing the relationships between subjects (users, group of users, processes on behalf of users, etc.) and objects (files, etc.). For example, both of them can answer the following two questions. The first question is "Given a subject, what objects can it access and how?" The second question is "Given an object, what subjects can access it and how?" For the first question, capabilities are the simplest way to answer while ACLs require all objects to be scanned; however, for the second question, ACLs are the simplest way while capabilities require all subjects to be scanned.

(3) Authorization table

Access table corresponds to storing the access matrix by items. It contains entries specifying which user or group of users has what access right to which object. Sorted on objects, it becomes to a set of ACLs; while sorted on subjects, it becomes a set of capabilities. Therefore it has the advantages of both ACLs and capabilities, and is more flexible than the above two. It is particular helpful for the access control in systems with sparse access matrixes.

Besides the three mechanisms introduced above, certain other mechanisms exist as well, such as ring-based access control, locks and keys, etc. Those access control mechanism can be used to enforced system security objectives, such as availability, integrity or confidentiality, by limiting access between methods and resources to collections of users or programs. Various techniques are utilized to implement those mechanisms.

3.3.3 *Audit and intrusion detection*

Audit is a posterior review of practices and events versus standards for purposes of evaluation and control. There are two types of audit: compliance audit and event audit. The definitions for compliance audit are different in different glossaries. We apply the definition from the E-Commerce PKI CA Glossary here that a "compliance audit is a review and examination of system records and activities in order to test for adequacy of system controls, to ensure compliance with established policy and operational procedures, to detect breaches in security, and to recommend any indicated changes in control, policy and procedures". Compliance audit can be classified into three common types further, which are regulatory audit, internal audit, and certified public accountant audit. Since compliance audit involves lots of social factors other than security itself, we will not go into its details here. Event audit is the process of gathering information about events happened in a system and analyzing the information to discover attacks to this system and reason about their causes. Event audit requires registration or logging of user requests and activities for later examination. Audit data is recorded in an audit trail or audit log, which varies from system to system. The auditing process can be performed both off-line and on-line. We will discuss event audit further below.

One important concept in event audit is intrusion detection. Intrusion detection is the process of monitoring the events occurring in a computer system or network and analyzing them for signs of intrusions, which are defined as attempts to compromise the confidentiality, integrity, availability of a resource, or to bypass the security mechanisms of a computer or network. Intrusion Detection Systems (IDSs) determine if actions perform intrusions base on one or more intrusion models. A model classifies a sequence of states or actions, or a characterization of states or actions, as "good" (no intrusion) or "bad" (possible intrusions). Modern IDSs primarily employ three models: misuse model, anomaly model and specification-based model.

Misuse detection characterizes a number of known attacks (misuse) to compromise a system and usually describes them as patterns or attack signatures, so the misuse detection is also called "signature-based intrusion detection". Misuse detection system monitors system events and is able to detect the explicit appearance or minor variations of know signatures. Misuse detection system requires a database of attack signatures and usually uses an expert system to identify intrusions based on a predetermined knowledge base. A misuse detection system has higher accuracy, but it could not detect any new intrusion without a pattern or signature. Therefore later IDSs use adaptive methods such as neural networks and Petri Nets to improve their detection abilities. For example, Kumar and Spafford [82] have adapted colored Petri Nets to detect both attack signatures and the actions following previously unknown attacks in their system Intrusion Detection In Our Time (IDIOT).

Anomaly detection uses the assumption that unexpected behavior is evidence of an intrusion. It requires determining a baseline of normal behavior. Then it is concerned with identifying events that appear to be anomalous with respect to normal system behaviors and reports when the computed results do not match the expected measurements. An anomaly detection system may use statistical, neural network, or data mining methods of analysis. Three different statistical models are used, which are threshold metric, statistical moment, and Markov model. For example, the Next-generation Intrusion Detection Expert System (NIDES) developed by SRI contains a statistical dynamic anomaly detector [1]. Anomaly detection can identify new and previously unseen attacks. But it is difficult to determine the boundary between acceptable and anomalous behavior at some time, so it will have higher false negative and false positive rates. And an experienced intruder could train an anomaly intrusion detection system gradually to accept an intrusion as normal behavior.

Specification based detection determines whether or not a sequence of intrusions violates a specification of how a program or system should execute. If so, it reports a potential intrusion[14]. Since the specification here is for security purpose, only those programs that may change the protection state of the system need to be specified and checked. Different from the misuse detection and anomaly detection, specification detection relies on traces or sequences of events and captures legitimate behaviors, not attack behaviors. Since it specifies the formalization of what should happen, it can detect intrusions using unknown attacks with low false alarms. However, extra efforts are needed to locate and analyze any program that may cause security problems in the system. Specification-based intrusion detection is still in its infancy. Ko, Ruschitzka, and Levitt [76] developed a specification-based intrusion detection system for the UNIX environment and applied it to monitoring program *rdist*. Uppuluri and Sekar [159] developed a declarative pattern language called Regular Expressions over Events (REE) and embedded REE into a rule-based language called Behavior Modeling Specification Language (BMSL), based on which they came up with a specification of a system and compiled the specification to produce a fast detection engine. Their experiences on 1999 Lincoln Labs offline evaluation data and 1999 AFRL online evaluation showed that this method could realize the promise of specification-based intrusion detection and was very effective.

3.3.4 *Cryptography*

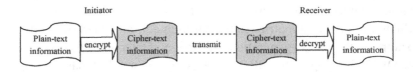

Figure 3 Cryptography

Cryptography is the technique of data encryption and decryption. It is widely used to protect secure-sensitive contents such as passwords, files, mutual communication, etc. When two entities need to talk or exchange some information, the initiator should encrypt the readable plain text into illegible cipher text. Then the cipher text is transmitted over the communication channel, which is most probably unsecured. When the receiver gets the cipher text, it decrypts it into readable plain text again. Figure 3 illustrates the cryptography process.

Encryption and decryption are based on certain algorithms and secrets, which are called "keys". It is desired that the choice of encrypt/decrypt algorithms and keys could satisfy the following requirements: encryption procedure is easy while any attempt to decrypt without the keys is difficult. According to the characteristics of keys, we can categorize cryptography into two main categories: symmetric cryptography and asymmetric cryptography [94].

(1) Symmetric Key Cryptography

Symmetric key cryptography is also called "shared-key cryptography" or "single-key cryptography". As indicated by the name, this kind of cryptography uses a common key for both encryption and decryption. Besides the initiator and the receiver, a Key Distribution Center (KDC) is often needed. The KDC sends secret keys through secure channels to the initiator, who encrypts the clear text to cipher text using the keys. On the receiver side, cipher text is decrypted using the same secret keys sent by the KDC and becomes clear text. Figure 4 illustrates this cryptography.

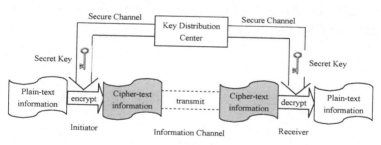

Figure 4 Symmetric Cryptography

Symmetric key cryptography has the advantages that the concept for symmetric key cryptography is simple and the parties involved in communications do not need to store the secret keys. A drawback of this kind of cryptography is that it requires large-scale distribution of the shared keys. So it is not suitable for very large distributed systems where building secure channels may be very expensive. In addition, it provides confidentiality of information but little authentication. Neither does it validate the integrity of the data transmitted.

(2) Asymmetric Cryptography

Asymmetric cryptography is also called "public key cryptography". In this kind of cryptography, two mathematically linked keys are applied. If one of them is used to encrypt some information, the other key must be used to decrypt the corresponding cipher text. One of the two keys is kept secret by a certain entity and is referred to as the "private key" of this entity. This private key represents the identity of its owner. The second key, which is called the "public key", is made available to the public. For instance, if the initiator Alice wants to send a message to receiver Bob, Alice will use the public key of Bob to encrypt this message and then sent the encrypted message to Bob. After Bob receives the encrypted message, he will decrypt it using his own private key. Since it is the assumption and requirement of asymmetric cryptography that it must be computationally infeasible to derive the private key from the public key, no one should be able to decrypt the message except for Bob. Therefore, asymmetric cryptography can provide authentication as well as confidentiality and integrity. Figure 5 illustrate the asymmetric cryptography.

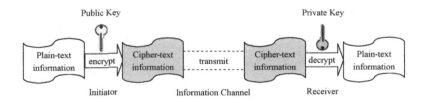

Figure 5 Asymmetric Cryptography

(3) Encryption/Decryption Algorithms

Encryption and decryption algorithms are the foundation on which any cryptography technique is built. Therefore they are of great importance.

Data Encryption Standard (DES) is a well-known symmetric key cryptography algorithm introduced in 1977 [23]. It encrypts data through confusion and diffusion. In this algorithm, blocks of 64 bits of data is encrypted and decrypted under the control of a 64 bit key. The encryption and decryption consist of 16 iterations; in each of which a separate key of 48-bit is used. The order in which the keys are used decides the process is an encryption or a decryption. Although DES has provided the impetus for many advances in the cryptography field and been the theoretical and practical groundwork for many other ciphers, it was broken in 1999. Its successor the Advanced Encryption Standard (AES) was proposed in 2001. The AES can use keys of 128, 192, or 256 bits and operates on blocks of 128 bits. It was specifically designed to withstand the attacks to which the DES showed weaknesses. At the same time, several other algorithms have been proposed to overcome the weaknesses in the DES, such as NewDES and IDEA.

RSA (Rivest Shamir Adelman) is a famous asymmetric cryptography algorithm and has universal acceptance. This algorithm has a strong theoretical foundation of RSA Problem (RSAP), which is conjectured to be equivalent to the Integer Factorization Problem (IFP). This problem is "given a positive integer n that is a product of two distinct odd primes p and q, a positive integer e such that $gcd(e, (p-1)(q-1)) = 1$, and an integer c, find an m such that m^e is congruent to $c \pmod{n}$." No easy method has been found for the RSAP problem yet. RSA has been widely used because it can provide data and origin authentication and non-repudiation in addition to confidentiality. For instance, Alice encrypts her message using her private key. Anyone can read it with Alice's public key. However, no one can alter this message without being noticed because the altered cipher-text message cannot be decrypted correctly using Alice's public key. So if the message can be decrypted correctly, we can guarantee that this message is really encrypted by Alice based on the assumption that Alice is the only one who knows her private key and the corresponding public key bearing her name really belongs to her. RSA can also be used to provide both confidentiality and authentication simultaneously, which requires encryption with the sender's private key and the recipient's public key.

3.3.5　*Firewall*

A firewall is considered as the first line of defense in protecting private information. A firewall is a set of related programs or hardware devices, located at a network gateway server, which protects the resources of a private network from other networks users by allowing and disallowing certain types of access on the basis of a configured security policy. The term also implies the security policy that is used with the programs. Firewall technology provides both physical and logical protection between different networks. A firewall is often installed in front of the rest of the network so that all information flowing into this network has to be checked by this firewall and cannot get directly at private network resources. An enterprise with an intranet that allows its workers access to the Internet installs a firewall to prevent outsiders from accessing its own private data resources and for controlling what outside resources its own users have access to. Firewalls fall into three broad categories: packet filters, proxy servers, and stateful multilayer inspection firewalls [41].

(1) Packet Filtering Firewalls

Packet filtering is the most basic form of firewall security. In a packet filtering firewall, each packet is compared to a set of established rule sets first. Depending on the comparison results, the firewall can drop the packet, forward it, or send a message to the originator. Rules can include source and destination IP address, source and destination port number and protocol used. So the header parts of packets often get examined. Packet filtering firewalls are usually part of a router firewall. A router is a device that receives packets from one network and forwards them to another. The advantage of packet filtering firewalls is their low cost and low impact on network performance. In addition, it has general and flexible structure, and provides extra security for the sub network. Most routers support packet filtering.

Packet filtering firewalls only work at the network layer. Although they are fairly effective and transparent to users, it is difficult to configure them. In addition, large sets of rules can be difficult to manage. Therefore, packet filtering firewalls by themselves do not support sophisticated rule based models and they are not adequate to secure a complex network from attacks. They are also susceptible to IP spoofing.

(2) Proxy Servers

A proxy server is a firewall component that acts as an intermediary between a LAN and the internet. It monitors a session instead of examining each packet. Once a session is established, all packets in that session are allowed to cross. It can be classified into three categories according to its working layer: circuit-level gateway, application-level gateway and stateful multilayer inspection firewalls.

Circuit-level gateways work at the session layer of the OSI model, or the TCP layer of TCP/IP. They monitor TCP handshaking between packets to determine whether a requested session is legitimate. Information passed to a remote computer through a circuit-level gateway appears to have originated from the gateway. This is useful for hiding information about the private network they protect. Circuit level gateways are relatively inexpensive. Besides security features, a circuit-level gateway can also act as an intermediary providing transparency to its users. When a user proposes a request, the circuit-level gateway receives it first. If the request passes filtering requirements, the circuit-level gateway looks in its local cache of previously downloaded contents. If the desired page is found, the circuit-level gateway returns it to the user directly instead of forwarding the request to the Internet. If it is not found, the circuit-level gateway acts as a client on behalf of the user and requests the page from the server on the Internet. When the page is returned, the circuit-level gateway relates it to the original request and forwards it to the user. Therefore an enterprise can ensure security, administrative control, and caching service by using a circuit-level gateway.

Application-level gateways can filter packets at the application layer of the OSI model and are application specific. Incoming or outgoing packets cannot access services for which there is no proxy. Because they examine packets at application layer, they can filter application specific commands, which cannot be accomplished by either packet filtering firewalls or circuit-level gateways. Application-level gateways can also be used to log user activities and logins. They offer a high level of security, but have a significant impact on network performance because context switches slow down network access dramatically. They are not transparent to end uses and require manual configuration of each client computer.

(3) Stateful Multilayer Inspection Firewalls

Stateful multilayer inspection firewalls are a hybrid combination of the other types of firewalls. They operate primarily on the network layer of the OSI model and transparently to the end users. They examine certain key parts of a packet and compare them with contents in a database of trusted information. According to the comparison results, they allow the packet to go through or discard it. They allow direct connection between client and host, alleviating the problem caused by the lack of transparency of application level gateways. They rely on algorithms to recognize and process application layer data instead of running application specific proxies. Stateful multiplayer inspection firewalls offer a high level of security, good performance and transparency to end users. However, they are expensive. In addition, if not administered by highly competent personnel, they are potentially less secure than simpler types of firewalls due to their complexity [41].

3.3.6 *Anti-virus software*

Anti-virus software is a class of software that looks for a virus or looks for indications of the presence of a virus in a data storage device, such as a hard drive, floppy disk, CD-ROM, etc, and prevents these programs from performing their functions. Since new viruses are created and dispatched all the time, some anti-virus software should be updated periodically. The market for anti-virus software has expanded because of Internet growth and the increasing use of the Internet by businesses concerned about protecting their computer assets. It is desired that more than one antivirus software packages are installed in a system, since no single product can do everything. There are three main kinds of anti-virus programs: scanners, monitors and integrity checkers [15].

Currently, scanners are the most popular and the most widely used anti-virus programs. They are programs that check for viruses by scanning the executable objects, such as executable files and boot sectors, for the presence of special code sequences or strings called "signatures". Each virus recognizable by scanners has a signature associated with it. Scanners mainly consist of a searching engine and a database of virus signatures. They are widely used because they are relatively easy to maintain and update. When a new virus appears, the authors of scanners just need to pick a good signature, which is present in each copy of the virus and at the same time is unlikely to be found in any legitimate program, and add the signature to the scanner's database. This is often done very quickly. In addition to scanning for virus signatures, some scanners go a step further. For instance, the "f-prot" from Frisk Software uses a heuristic analyzer to see if executable objects contain virus-like code, such as time-triggered events, and software load trapping. Heuristics is a relatively new, but effective way to find viruses without defined signatures yet. Scanning techniques have some other variations, like virus removal programs, resident scanners, virus identifiers, and etc.

Monitors are memory resident programs, which continuously monitor computer's memory, automatically detect, and remove viruses without interrupting users' works. Once a program tries to use a function, which is considered to be dangerous and virus-like, the monitoring program intercepts it and either denies it completely or asks the user for confirmation. Unlike the scanners, the monitors are not virus-specific and therefore need not to be constantly updated. But monitors have two main drawbacks which make them weaker than the scanners. One drawback is that monitors can be bypassed by the so-called "tunneling" viruses which attempt to follow the interrupt chain back down to the basic DOS or BIOS interrupt handlers and then install themselves. The other drawback is that monitors try to detect a virus by its behavior, which may cause many false alarms since viruses may use functions similar to those used by the normal programs.

Integrity checkers are programs which read the entire disk, compute some kind of checksum of the executable code in a computer system, and store the checksum in a database. The integrity checkers re-compute the checksum periodically and compare it with the stored original value to detect whether the executable code in this system have been modified. There are three main kinds of integrity checkers. The most widely used one is the off-line integrity checker, which checks the integrity of all the executable code in a computer system. Another kind is the integrity module. It can be attached to an executable file, which can check its integrity when starting its execution. The third kind is the integrity shell. It is a resident program which checks the integrity of an object only when this object is about to be executed. Integrity checkers are not virus-specific and do not need constant updating like the scanners. Currently, they are the most cost-effective and sound line of defense against the computer viruses. However, integrity checkers can only detect and report viruses, but cannot block them from infecting other files or systems. They usually cannot determine the source of infection either. Since the original checksum is considered to be the correct one for later comparison, integrity checkers must be initially installed in a virus-free system. In addition, they are prone to false positive alerts since changes they detected may be legitimate changes of a certain program. Although integrity checkers have those drawbacks mentioned above, their future is predicted as bright by specialists [15].

Chapter 4

Security Issues in a Mobile Agent System

We have already introduced a mobile agent system in Chapter 2. Based on the basic concepts and primary features of a mobile agent system, we can derive possible security issues in such a mobile agent system and corresponding security requirements for a generic secure mobile agent system. In this chapter, after introducing the security-related features and security measures taken in a representative subset of existing mobile agent systems, we summarized the research work devoted to the security of a mobile agent system.

4.1 Security Issues in a Mobile Agent System

4.1.1 *Possible attacks to a mobile agent system*

There might be many different kinds of attacks to a mobile agent system. Since a mobile agent system mainly consists of mobile agents and mobile agent platforms, most attacks are towards these two main entities. We will introduce the attacks to them respectively in the following.

4.1.1.1 *Possible attacks to a mobile agent*

A mobile agent has to expose its own information to the platform it migrates to so that it could be executed. In the case of strong migration, it has to expose its code, data and state. In the case of strong mobility, its code and data have to be exposed. Due to this fact, a mobile agent faces more severe security risks. A malicious platform can try to attack it in different ways. If we consider the home platform environment to be the totally secure environment and try to achieve such a protection level for a mobile agent in other platform, we can identify the following possible attacks of a malicious platform.

Leak out/Modify mobile agent's code

The mobile agent's code has to be readable by a guest platform. This characteristic makes the attack of leaking out/modifying mobile agent's code unavoidable. A malicious platform could read and remember the instruction going to be executed and might infer the rest of the program based on that knowledge. Thus the platform could get to know the strategy and purpose of the mobile agent. The situation becomes worse if the mobile agent represents a class of mobile agents or is generated out of standard building libraries. Therefore a malicious platform can have a complete picture of a number of mobile agents' behavior. If the malicious platform infers the physical address and has access to the code memory, it can modify the agent's code either directly or through inserting some vicious part like a virus. It could also change the code temporarily to avoid being detected by modifying the code, executing the code modified and resuming the original code before the mobile agent leaves.

Leak out/Modify mobile agent's data

This could be very dangerous too. Since some data are security sensitive, such as security keys, electronic cash, or social security numbers, it may cause leak of privacy or loss of money. If a malicious platform knows the physical location of data, it may modify the data in accordance with the semantics of data. Therefore it can result in very severe consequences. In some cases, even if the data being leaked is not that sensitive, a malicious platform can still take advantage of those data and perform attack. For example, if a malicious platform gets to know the traveling date of a person, it may leak it to some thief.

Leak out/Modify mobile agent's execution flow

If a malicious platform knows a mobile agent's code, data and the physical location of its program counter, it can infer what instruction will be executed next. Moreover, it can deduce the state of that mobile agent. Then it might change the execution flow according to its will to achieve its goal. For example, it may find that the mobile agent first compares the price of a product or service provided by the platform with the expected price of the agent itself, and decides to use it or not afterwards. A malicious platform might force the mobile agent to ignore the result of the comparison and accept its product or service directly by making the execution flow jump to some point. A malicious platform can also take advantage of its ability to modify the mobile agent's execution to deliberately execute agent's code in a wrong way.

Denial of service

A malicious platform can simply not execute the mobile agent migrating to it or put the agent into waiting list and thus cause delay to that mobile agent. It is also an attack to the mobile agent since it may make the mobile agent miss some good chances if the agent can finish its execution on that platform in time and travel to other platforms.

Masquerade

A malicious platform may disguise itself as a platform to which a mobile agent will migrate to or even as the home platform when the mobile agent returns. If it succeeds, it can get the secrets of the mobile agent by cheating and at the same time hurt the reputation of the original platform. For example, a malicious platform may pretend to be an airline company and give a mobile agent a fake ticket after it gets the money. But the mobile agent doesn't really get the ticket and may have dispute with the real airline company later.

Leak out/Modify the interaction between a mobile agent and other parties

A malicious platform may eavesdrop on the interaction between a mobile agent and other parties like another agent or another platform. From the information it gets, it may infer some secrets about the mobile agent and the third party. Moreover, if it can alternate the content of the interaction, or disguise itself as part of the interaction, or direct the interaction to another unexpected third party, it may perform attacks to the mobile agent and the third party as well.

4.1.1.2 *Possible attacks to a mobile agent platform*

A mobile agent platform provides the execution and communication environment for incoming mobile agents. A malicious mobile agent may exploit the security weaknesses of a mobile agent platform or launch attacks against the platform. The possible attacks include the following [64][39].

Masquerade

A malicious mobile agent may claim itself as another agent on a mobile agent platform. Such masquerading action can also be called "faking". The aim of masquerading of a malicious agent is either to fake as an authorized agent so as to gain access to the services and resources of this mobile agent platform which are not assigned to it; or to fake as another unauthorized agent so as to find a "scapegoat" and shift the blame and punishment of any malicious actions it will conduct. The results of masquerading include unauthorized access and even damage to platform resources, leaking confidential secrets, and ruining the established trust and reputation of the legitimate agent.

Denial of Service

The denial of service attack to a mobile agent platform may be from a malicious mobile agent that deliberately exploits system vulnerabilities or a mobile agent written with programming errors unintentionally. But the consequences are similar. The "bad" mobile agents consume an excessive amount of the resources of this mobile agent platform, degrade the performance of the platform, make the platform unavailable to other legitimate agents, or even completely terminate the platform or shut it down.

Unauthorized Access

If a mobile agent platform is not equipped with an authorization mechanism, or such mechanism fails for a malicious agent that takes advantage of the vulnerability of the platform, a malicious agent may have unauthorized access to the resources of the platform. Not only the privacy and integrity of this platform may be detrimentally affected, but also other mobile agents would be attacked from a variety of aspects, which in turn will have a negative impact on the entire mobile agent system.

Obviously, those attacks are dangerous and harmful to mobile agent systems. In order to avoid those attacks, a secure mobile agent system must satisfy the following requirements.

4.1.2 *Security requirements for a secure mobile agent system*

Many researchers discussed the security issues in a mobile agent system from different aspects. Chess et. al. summarized the assumptions violated by mobile agent systems that underlie most existing computer security implementations, such as the identification of programs with persons. Some security issues, arising in mobile agent system with new features such as authentication, reputation and trust, are pointed out, as well as some of the addressing ways [26]. Farmer, Jansen, Rothermel and etc. analyzed mobile agent system overviewed the threats and security problems, and identified generic security objectives and requirements separately in [36][64][128].

We generalize several security requirements for a secure mobile agent system in the following based on the similarity of problems to be addressed. It is quite possible that a security issue we mentioned above may fall into more than one requirement. Also a solution to the problem of one area would be the solution to another requirement area. Our division aims to break a huge security problem into sub problems that could be handled more easily [112].

Authentication and Authorization

Both a mobile agent and a platform need to authenticate the identity of the other part. *Authentication* of an entity is the process of verifying the identity or other relevant information about the entity. At one level, the problem of authentication in mobile agent system is very similar to the problem of authentication in distributed systems in general. But on the other hand, some of the known difficulties with standard authentication systems are even more serious in mobile agent systems. The outcome of the authentication processes is that the user/agent knows the identity of the server/agent execution environment and the server/agent execution environment knows the identity of the user/agent. The process of deciding whether or not to grant a request after confirmation about the authentication of the principal is called *authorization* or *access control*. To achieve those security properties, digital signatures may be required in addition to password access.

Privacy and Confidentiality

The privacy requirement includes problems of confidentiality of exchanges and interactions in a mobile agent system. In many transactions, entities require that only the parties involved have access to the information communicated in the transaction. In addition, it may be desirable to prevent external entities from gaining access to identities of the parties involved or to the information being accessed. Additionally, since the platform is in charge of the entire state of a mobile agent, mechanisms must be provided to allow privacy of the information being accumulated in and carried by the agent to other platforms.

Non-Repudiation

The problem of repudiation arises when a party involved in a communication or an activity later denies its involvement. Important communication exchanges must be logged to prevent later denials by any party to a transaction. If a mobile agent platform and a mobile agent commit to a digital agreement, contract, sale, or other such transaction, then it must be highly provable that such commitment was made by both sides.

Accountability

Each process, human user, or agent on a given platform must be held accountable for their actions. In order to achieve this purpose, we need to record not only unique identification and authentication, but also an audit log of security relevant events and the agent or process responsible for those events. Security relevant events are predefined by mobile agent platforms' security policies. Generally speaking, security related activities must be recorded for auditing and tracing purposes. Audit logs must be protected from unauthorized access and modification as well.

Availability

This requirement should be ensured for both data and services of a mobile agent platform to local agents and incoming mobile agents. A mobile agent platform must be able to provide controlled concurrency, support for simultaneous access, deadlock management, and exclusive access as required. Shared data must be available in a usable form; capacity must be available to meet service needs, and provisions of the fair allocation of resources and timeliness of service must be made. An agent platform must also be able to detect and recover from system software and hardware failures. An agent platform should also have the ability to deal with big amounts of visiting and accessing to avoid denial-of-service attacks.

Anonymity

The security policies of agent platforms and their auditing requirements must be carefully balanced with agent privacy expectations. The platform may be able to keep the agent's identity secret from other agents and still maintain anonymity where it can determine the agent's identity if necessary and legal.

Fairness

Fairness property requires that no party gain an advantage over other parties. In a mobile agent system, mechanisms are necessary to ensure fair agent-platform interaction in electronic exchange.

4.2   Related Works

4.2.1 *Existing mobile agent systems*

Over the years, a number of mobile agent systems have been developed and applied. Our thesis does not intend to survey these systems comprehensively and thoroughly. What we want to do is to provide an overview on the security-related features and security measures taken in a representative subset of these systems. Mobile agent systems with little security support, such as Messengers [105] and Obliq, will be ignored in the following. Most of these existing mobile agent systems do not have formal methods as their basis to verify their security claims. Therefore proposing a formal framework for a generic mobile agent system is a common desire. We believe that considering the security features and mechanisms in these system helps with the design of such a generic formal model.

Agent Tcl/D'Agents

Agent Tcl [50] is developed in Dartmouth College. It allows mobile agents implemented in secure languages such as Safe-Tcl and Java to migrate in the network. When a mobile agent migrates, its entire source code, data and execution state is transferred. A mobile agent can also be cloned and dispatched to the desired machine. Agent Tcl security model distinguishes two kinds of agents: Authenticated agent and Anonymous agent. The former are agents created and/or cloned by authenticated user. Each server maintains a list of authorized users. Agent Tcl uses asymmetric ciphered algorithms, typically RSA, for agent and user authentication in conjunction with PGP (Pretty Good Privacy) systems. The latter are foreign agents which will be executed with restricted rights. A server can be configured to accept or decline anonymous agent execution. For access control, Agent Tcl platform implements a discretionary right model in conjunction with Safe Tcl for doubt script running control.

The successor of Agent Tcl is D'Agents [51] which supports multi-languages. D'Agents can automatically capture and restore the complete state of a migrating agent. D'Agents [52] server uses public-key cryptography to authenticate the identity of the owner of an incoming mobile agent to verify that the mobile agent is from the host that it claims to be from. The public-key cryptography also prevents a mobile agent from being intercepted. After authentication is successful, the mobile agent is granted access rights by stationary resource-manager agents. But most resource manager agents are consulted only when the mobile agent attempts to access the corresponding resource or explicitly requests a specific access right. These access rights are enforced by language specific enforcement modules. The access control lists are usually at a coarse granularity, which means mobile agents coming from a specific machine are subjected to the same access rules.

Aglet

Aglet [70] of IBM is one of the first Mobile agent systems using Java technology. It uses the Java serialization facility to transfer a mobile agent, which is called an *aglet* in the system, together with its state among agent servers, which are called *aglet contexts*. It should be noted that the "state" does not include an agent's thread state because it is not supported by the standard Java virtual machine. Aglets use an event driven model, called *callback* model. When a certain event occurs for a mobile agent, such as arriving on a new machine, the corresponding method of this mobile agent is invoked by the system.

The concept of agent server or aglet context is also used for Aglet's security support. An authentication mechanism is implemented between aglet contexts. The authentication is mainly based on MAC (Message Authentication Code). When an aglet arrives at a context, it is authenticated based on its owner and manufacturer. Aglet contexts trust each other if and only if they belong to the same server domain. Authentication between distant contexts from different domains is based on trusted certification process. Based on the authentication result, an aglet is assigned a set of permissions, which are enforced with standard Java security mechanism. This security model is similar to that of the D'Agent. The resource access control is implemented by a database permission that clearly specifies agent access rights on different resources. In addition, Aglet offers the possibility to define a specific security policy for each agent. This policy is encoded within the Aglet process.

Ajanta

Ajanta [71], also written in Java, is developed at the University of Minnesota. It addresses both the system level issues such as mobility, global naming and security, and the language-level support for agent programming including models and primitives.

The Ajanta architecture includes a generic agent server which provides a secure agent execution environment. Agents are isolated within *protection domains*, created using features of the Java environment. In Ajanta, mobile agent transfer is encrypted and authenticated using the ElGamal and DSA protocols, the resource access are based on capability, and authorization is based on agent's owner. It also provides mechanisms to detect tampering of agent state and code.

Ara

Ara [122] stands for "Agents for Remote Action" and is developed by University of Kaiserslautern. It is a multi-language mobile agent system supporting agents written in TCL, Java and C/C++. It supports strong mobility and also allows a mobile agent to *checkpoint* its current internal state at any time during its execution. The entire Ara system is multi-threaded with TCL, Java and MACE interpreters together with the agent server running inside a single UNIX process. When a new mobile agent arrives at a host, a new thread begins to execute it. Agent communications are communications between threads. This feature brings performance advantages.

In security aspect, the *places* existing on an Ara system play the central role. An Ara place establishes a *domain* of logically related services under a common security policy governing all agents at that place. The central function of a place is to decide on the conditions of admission of an agent applying to enter. These conditions are expressed in the form of *allowance*. A mobile agent code is signed by its writer, while its arguments and overall resource allowance signed by its user. When a mobile agent resumes its execution after a successful migration and admission procedure which involves authentication, it may check its local allowance and discover to what extent the place has honored its desires.

Concordia

Concordia [171][177] is created by Mitsubishi Electronic Information Center America. It is also a Java-based mobile agent system. Like most other Java-based mobile agent systems, Concordia provides agent mobility using Java's serialization and class loading mechanisms, but does not support state capture at the thread level. An *itinerary* object, which includes the mobile agent's migration path and the methods to be executed at each agent server, is bundled with each mobile agent.

Concordia has a strong focus on security and reliability. It includes three security features: access control, reliable agent transport, and cipher A mobile agent is encrypted when it is in migration or is in persistent stores to avoid being tampered. An agent server uses cryptographic authentication of a mobile agent's owner to be protected from malicious mobile agents. Concordia supports a lot of standard encryption tools and protocols such as SSLv3 and JCE APIs to implement encryption algorithms such as IDEA, DES, RC4, and RC5. The resources on a mobile agent server are protected by a statically-specified access control list based on user identities. Each agent is securely associated with a particular user, and carries a one-way hash value of that user's password. Those agents inherit their users' access rights. Concordia also uses a Queue Manager in conjunction with a two-phase commit transfer protocol to allow agent mobility even when the target host is down.

Jumping Beans

Jumping Beans [1] developed by Jumping Beans Inc. is also based on Java. Strictly speaking, it is not a mobile agent framework because it is focused strictly on mobility and security. But it could be a framework to build a mobile agent system with less worry about the details of mobility and security. On a receiving computer, a Jumping Beans daemon resides and runs to facilitate receiving a jumping application and enforce security afterwards.

Jumping Beans has four layers of security, which include *traditional distributed security* layer which claims to employ all of the standard security techniques used in traditional distributed computing systems; *multi-jump security* layer which can assign a fine-grained level of trust to each host; *trusted source* layer which ensures the code executed by a jumping application comes from a known trusted source even if the jumping application was launched by an untrusted host or has visited an untrusted host; and *monitoring and intervention* layer which can help with tracking the activity in the entire system to detect unwanted one and control jumping applications to prevent or stop unwanted activity. It uses a centralized server architecture that a jumping application must pass through from one machine to another. This feature simplifies security management as well as tracking. But it becomes a performance bottleneck.

Mole

Mole [139] is a project at the University of Stuttgart. It also uses Java for mobility support and security. An agent in Mole is the transitive closure of objects that reference each other. To communicate with other agents or the host environment, agents make use of symbolic reference similar to aglet proxies.

TACOMA

TACOMA [67][68] is the abbreviation of Tormsø And Cornell Moving Agents, which is a joint project of the University of Tormsø and Cornell University. When a mobile agent is going to move, it must create *folders* to store its code and any desired state information. Folders are then aggregated into *briefcases* and sent to the new machine. On the new machine, the mobile agent communicates with or get executed by a local agent by using the *meet* primitive. As automatic state-capture facilities are not supported in TACOMA, an agent programmer should be responsible for capturing the agent state.

The original TACOMA does not implement security mechanism. It relies on the underlying operating system for security. But later TACOMA provides hooks for adding a cryptographic authentication subsystem to reject agents from untrusted parties. It also uses a firewall type mechanism between the agent execution and the host system to protect the host from malicious agents. Security automata is used to specify a machine's security policy and enforce the policy. Fault tolerance of TACOMA is achieved by using replication and *rear guard*, which is a clone of a mobile agent left on the last site that the agent visited.

Telescript/Odyssey

Telescript [149][174] is the first commercial mobile agent system, which is developed by General Magic. In Telescript, a server runs on each network site which maintains one or more virtual *places*. The place authenticates the identity of an incoming mobile agent's owner by examining the agent's *cryptographic credentials*. An agent passed the authentication is then assigned a set of access rights or *permits* by the place. Once attempting to violate its permits, a mobile agent is terminated immediately. In this model, the Telescript places are safe from agents. With the overwhelming success of Java, Telescript was drowned from the market and reimplemented in Java as Odyssey [175] with much of the original paradigm preserved. As in Telescript, the notion of security in Odyssey has been included in the design of the object-oriented source language, Java. The class hierarchy includes certain semantic limitations. For example, a class can be sealed such that it may not be extended or subtyped; a class can be abstracted such that it is not able to be instantiated; pointers can be turned into *protected references* such that an object may not be modified by accessing it through a protected reference. The last one helps with building a sort of *read-only* capability in the system.

Although Telescript was viewed as one of the most secure, fault-tolerant and efficient mobile agent systems, its weak security aspects have been pointed out in [152] as "suffered from a lack of systematic design and not clear how to be convinced of the consistency of the implemented security restrictions".

Voyager

Voyager [115], which is another Java-based mobile agent system, is developed by ObjectSpace. It provides the same basic security mechanisms as other Java based systems. In Voyager, two kinds of objects are defined: *native objects* and *external objects*. Native objects are considered as trusted objects since they have been loaded by a local class. Such objects have a total control on resources and can access all execution context objects. External objects are considered as untrusted objects, and therefore can only access resource based on access control policies.

From the above discussion about the existing mobile agent systems, we can see that most mobile agent systems are developed using Java and their security mechanisms mainly rely on the Java features. And little of them base the development on formal methods which supports formal analysis and verification.

4.2.2 *Security research*

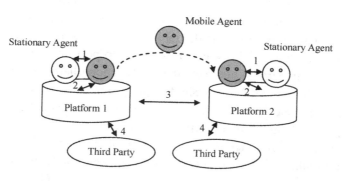

Figure 6 Security Areas in a Mobile Agent System

Overview of the existing mobile agent systems above shows that many conventional security techniques used in contemporary distributed applications have also played a role in the mobile agent paradigm. Moreover, various extensions to those conventional techniques are available. But due to the unique characteristics of a mobile agent system, some special countermeasures should be created. In a generic mobile agent system, four security areas can be identified as illustrated in Figure 6, namely: (1) inter-agent security; (2) agent-platform security; (3) inter-platform security; and (4) security between platforms and unauthorized third parties [128]. Many security problems in areas (1), (3) and (4) have counterparts in conventional client-server systems. Existing cryptographic technologies seem to be applicable to such security problems. But area (2) is special and particularly important to a mobile agent system.

When the relationship between a mobile agent and a mobile agent platform is considered, two security sub-areas can be identified. On the one hand, mobile agent platforms should be protected from attacks from malicious agents. This is known as "host security" or "mobile agent platform security." On the other hand, mobile agents should be protected from being tampered with by malicious mobile agent platforms. This is known as "code security" or "mobile agent security". Since a mobile agent consists of code, data and state, and all of them are under possible attacks; we prefer to use "mobile agent security" instead of "code security" for clarity. Mobile agent security is notoriously difficult as a mobile agent has to expose its three areas mentioned above to a mobile agent platform. If the mobile agent platform is malicious, it can take advantage of this kind of exposure to perform various attacks. It was once generally believed that only under hardware protection could a mobile agent be protected [26]. Recent advances of research works in this field have shown the incorrectness of this belief, although techniques and methods are still in great need to solve this problem. Research in mobile agent security area always includes detection, prevention and their miscellaneous. Mobile agent platform security and mobile agent security are not isolated from each other. On the contrary, they are closely related, especially during the mobile agent migration. Figure 7 illustrates the mobile agent system security research areas.

Figure 7 Mobile Agent System Security Research Areas

4.2.2.1 *Security measures for a mobile agent platform*

A mobile agent platform is vulnerable to attacks from many sources as introduced in section 4.1. Since a mobile agent platform in a mobile agent system is similar to a server in the traditional client-server environment, fortunately many conventional security techniques for client-server environment could act as countermeasures to protect the agent platform. The main ideas of protecting a mobile agent platform from attacks should include the following three aspects. First, a safe environment should be provided for execution of any alien program, which includes both software-based fault isolation and safe-code interpretation. Second, the safety properties of any alien code should be checked before being executed on the platform. And third, the security should be ensured through signed code and path histories.

To provide a safe environment for execution of any alien program, conventional security techniques help with supporting several mechanisms including the following [64]:

1) Mechanisms to isolate processes from one another and from the control process, which allow untrusted programs written in unsafe languages to be executed safely within the single virtual address space of an application;
2) Mechanisms to control access to computational resources;
3) Cryptographic methods to encrypt information exchanges;
4) Cryptographic methods to identify and authenticate users, agents, and platforms;
5) Mechanisms to audit security relevant events occurring on the agent platform.

Similarly, more recently developed techniques which aim at mobile code and are applicable to mobile agent security have evolved along those same traditional directions. They include the following:

1) Developing agents using an interpreted script or programming language, which facilitates the support for mobile agent platforms on heterogeneous computer systems as well as the development of the agent code;

2) Limiting the capabilities of agent languages so that they are considered "safe";
3) Applying digital signatures to agents and other information to indicate authenticity;
4) Restricting an agent's capabilities on an agent platform by constraining resources (e.g., lifetime, storage), controlling service access (e.g., network destinations, directory segment) and making capabilities location dependent.

"Sandbox" in Java and "padded cell'" in Agent TCL are real world security mechanisms in the first aspect. Java programming language and runtime environment illustrate the nature of the recently developed techniques listed above. The Java environment includes built-in security controls such as "sandbox" model for isolation of code into mutually exclusive execution domains, in which untrusted code is executed under a watchful eye of a security manager. Thus all potentially dangerous procedure calls are restricted by special security control components that decide which programs can use these procedures and which cannot. The security manager is the master piece in the JVM and operating system security. It determines most of the parameters of the Java sandbox. The existence of a key database is used by the security manager to verify the digital signature included in a signed class. Java environment also has the "byte code" verifier to perform static and dynamic analysis of the program to guarantee that the current byte code corresponds to a valid Java program. The byte code verification can check the safety of class file downloads. The Java security model for version 1.2 contains a new permission-based mechanism for constraining the computational capabilities of mobile code, which can also benefit agent systems based on Java. Each permission specifies the authorized access to a particular resource, such as a connect permission to allow access to a given host and port. The Java Cryptography Architecture (JCA) introduces the notion of a Cryptography Package Provider. The Aglet security model, for example, to a large degree reflects Java's underlying protection mechanisms. However, Java has limitations to account for memory, CPU and network resources consumed by individual threads. It does not support thread mobility (strong mobility) either.

Safe TCL, the best known of the safe interpreters for script-based languages, employs a "padded cell" concept as a counterpart to Java's sandbox [64]. The term "padded cell" denotes an isolation technique whereby a second interpreter pre-screens any harmful commands from being executed by the main interpreter. The term padded cell refers to this isolation and access control technique, which provides the foundation for implementing the reference monitor concept. More than one safe interpreter can be used to implement different security policies, if needed. Similar mechanisms to those in Java for constraining agents have been built into Agent TCL, Telescript and Odyssey.

The second aspect is to check the safety properties of any alien code before executing it on the platform. Necula and Lee proposed the Proof Carrying Code (PCC) approach [107][108][109]. They described the design and a typical implementation of PCC, where the language used for specifying the safety properties is first-order predicate logic. PCC enables a computer system to determine automatically and with certainty that program code provided by another system is safe to install and execute without requiring interpretation or run-time checking.

It should be the responsibility of the code writer to formally prove that the program possesses safety properties required by the code executer. The code with its proof is sent to the code executer, usually a mobile agent platform, to get verified. The proof is in a form which does not require cryptographic techniques or external assistance to verify it. To ensure that the attached proof really corresponds to the code, a safety predicate representing the semantics of the program is generated directly from the native code. As long as the proof is verified, the corresponding code can be executed with no need for further checking.

The third aspect is to ensure the security through signed code and path histories. It is a fundamental method to sign a mobile agent using a digital signature to protect it from tampering and thus ensure the mobile agent platform security. Code signing aims at confirming the authenticity of an object, its origin as well as its integrity. It uses public key cryptography, which involves a pair of keys associated with an entity [94]. One of the keys is held and used for encrypting a mobile agent by the sender platform, and the other is held and used to decrypt this mobile agent by the receiver platform. The former key is usually the private key of the sender while the latter key is usually the public key of the sender. A digital signature is formed by computing a non-reversible hash value of the agent's code and then encrypting this value (called fingerprint or message digest) using the private key. Because of the uniqueness of the fingerprint, it works as an integrity mechanism as well as an authentication mechanism. Then the digital signature is associated with the agent's code it signs. The association can be handled differently, such as in Communicator 4.x and Mozilla.

It is also helpful for the security of mobile agent platforms that a mobile agent maintains a record of the platforms it has already visited. So a new platform this mobile will visit can take advantage of this record to determine whether to accept and process this agent and what resource constraints to apply. Such a platform record has one entry for each platform visited. Each entry should include the identifiers of this platform and the next platform to be visited, and be signed using a fingerprint computed based on the previous path history. This path history is then provided to a new platform once this mobile agent arrives on it. This platform checks this path history first by either reviewing all identifiers, or authenticating each signature of each platform entry individually. Based on this result, the new platform can determine whether it should trust the mobile agent's previous platforms and determine whether and how to execute this mobile agent afterwards. The path history technique cannot prevent a platform from being malicious to mobile agent and other mobile agent platforms, but it can act as a deterrent.

4.2.2.2 *Security measures for a mobile agent*

Protecting mobile agents is a relatively new topic and commonly agreed difficult area in the security society. The home platform of a mobile agent, which creates and launches this mobile agent, is usually considered to be the most secure environment for that agent. Once a mobile agent leaves its home platform, it might travel in a trusted network or an unfamiliar environment. Platforms that a mobile agent migrates to could tamper with the agent's code, data, or state to disclose private information, gain advantages over other platforms, or "brainwash" the agent for their own purposes. This problem is particularly challenging due to the difficulty of protecting a program from the processor which executes the program. Several researchers have worked on this problem and proposed their security measures. Based on our survey, there are six main directions listed below in this area.

The first direction is the organizational approach applied by General Magic Inc. It eliminates the problem by allowing only trustworthy institutions to run mobile agent systems. This security mechanism stems more from the viewpoint that hardware protects software. Although it may be a secure way to protect a mobile agent system, it cannot support an open system [26].

The second direction is the trust/reputation approach proposed by Farmer, Guttmann and Swarup [35][36]. They discussed achievable security goals for mobile agents and proposed an architecture to achieve those goals. A unique point of their work is a specific mechanism called "state appraisal," which protects users and hosts from attacks via state modifications. This mechanism also provides users with flexible control over the authority of their agents. Their mechanism focuses on the state information and makes efforts to prevent the mobile agent's state from being modified by other parties. But this mechanism cannot detect the situation in which a mobile agent's code is modified.

The third is the manipulation detection approach developed by Vigna [166][167]. His method is based on "cryptographic tracing" which can detect manipulations of agent data or the execution of code. The proposed method does not require dedicated tamper-proof hardware of trust between parties. But this mechanism might produce traces with huge size. Cryptographic tracing has been extended by Tan and Moreau [146][147] to protect mobile code from denial-of-service and state tampering attacks. They introduced a trusted third party, the verification server, to undertake the verification of execution traces on behalf of the agent owner. They used model checking method to verify the security properties of their protocol.

The blackbox protection approach is the forth direction which is created by Hohl [57][58][59]. This method aims to generate a blackbox out of agent code by using code obfuscating techniques. Since the attackers must spend some time to analyze the blackbox code before they perform attacks, this mechanism can protect a mobile agent from most of the attacks for a certain interval. After that period, the agent itself and the data it transported will become invalid so as to avoid attacks. But the security mechanism costs extra time when a mobile agent is created, transmitted, and executed.

The Computing with Encrypted Functions (CEF) approach is the fifth and put forwarded by Sander and Tschudin [131][132][133]. They used encrypted functions and the method of hiding the signing function to make digital signatures "undetectable." In this way, they can prevent the abuse of signing procedure from signing arbitrary documents. They only identified a special class of functions - polynomials and rational functions. There is still a gap between those functions and general programs. Kotzanikolaou et. al. extended the CEF approach and proposed a RSA-based method to solve the open problem on undetachable signatures in Sander and Tschudin's work [79].

The above works solve some of the problems in mobile agent security from different perspectives. However, neither of them has a formal method as its basis. Therefore, it is not easy to prove or analyze the characteristics of the mobile agent systems using these techniques based on formal means. The sixth direction aims to take advantage of the benefits provided by formal method and solve the mobile agent security problems formally. SEAL Calculus is one example in this direction. The SEAL calculus is based on π-calculus and is extended by Vitek et. al for distribution, mobility and security [168][169]. It incorporates a strong resource access control based on linear revocable capabilities called portals and enforces a hierarchical protection model. A mobile agent platform controls all external resources used by its resident agents, while agents can protect themselves from their platforms by controlling visibility and access to their own resources. Although the security properties which can be proven in [168][169] only relate to protection of the mobile agent platform from the malicious actions of mobile agents, it was claimed that a protocol would be devised to provide some guarantees to mobile computations as well.

All the works we mentioned above are concern with the secure execution of a mobile agent in a hostile environment, which is an important part of mobile agent security. At the same time, another critical part should also be considered. That is the secure mobile agent migration, or secure mobility, which affects both mobile agent platform security and mobile agent security as a powerful shield.

4.2.3 *Mobility modeling*

To solve the security problems in a mobile agent system including both secure execution and secure mobility, a model of a mobile agent system is needed first. Designing and modeling mobile agent systems have become an active topic. Since mobility is the most distinct characteristic of a mobile agent, mobility modeling also attracts much attention. There are two kinds of mobility in the distributed computing area: physical mobility and logical mobility. For mobile agent mobility, we usually refer to the latter. Many mobile agent system models have been developed by several academic and industrial research groups. They utilized different modeling tools and environments, and their mobile agent system modeling has different features. According to the underlying basis of those models, we can categorize those models into three categories.

Models and systems in the first category directly use programming languages like Java. Features of Java, like the class serialization, are utilized for modeling mobility. One example in this category is the JAMES (Java-Based Agent Modeling Environment for Simulation) developed by Uhrmacher, et. al.[157][158]. It realizes variable structure models including mobility from the perspective of single autonomous agents. It reuses and combines concepts of distributed systems and parallel DEVS with ideas of endomorphy and variable structure modeling. Mobility modeling of an agent is represented by making it disappear in one location and reappear in another location with the same internal state and identity. This process starts with a message created by an atomic model B willing to move, in which B asks another atomic model C located remotely to add it to the coupled model C is in. We argue that this method overlooks the period while a mobile agent is during its travel and leaves little space for security consideration for the entire system, especially for secure mobility. Also this method does not reflect the real world quite appropriately with respect to the transparency of a mobile agent's knowledge about the remote structure in a network. In addition, this method is not formal and hard for analysis of system features.

The second category is based on pure mathematical methods and calculi. Kim et. al. proposed canonical stochastic models of mobile agent behavior which includes modeling of agent dwell time, agent lifespan, cloning scenarios, inter-report processes, etc. several statistical and mathematical models of mobile agents are developed and mobile agent functions are categorized [73]. Another example in the second category is to use the Seal Calculus we mentioned in section 4.2.2.2. From one aspect, Seal can be roughly described as the "π"-calculus with hierarchical locations, mobility and resource access control. From another aspect, Seal is as a substrate for implementing higher level languages and advanced distributed services. Seals may be moved over channels. And by proposing several mechanisms for security defense, secure mobile agent system could be written. Although the security properties proven in [168][169] only relate to protecting a platform, it was claimed that a protocol would be devised to provide some guarantees to mobile computations as well. Ambient Calculus by Cardelli and Gordon [21][47] is another example, which is a concurrent calculus where the unifying notion of "ambient" is used to model many different constructs for distributed and mobile computation. Its emphasis is on boundaries and their effects on computation. Security is represented as the ability or inability to cross boundaries. Mobile UNITY by Picco and Roman [123][125] differs from the above approaches mainly in the form that Mobile UNITY is essentially state-based and has a notation closer to the one of a conventional programming language. Since models in this category are formal, they support rigid formal analysis. But they lack intuitiveness and are usually not easy to read. In addition, extensions to the calculi may affect the existing model to a considerable extent.

The third category is to use intuitive graphical formalism like Petri Nets and various extended Petri Nets. Petri Nets have a so-called "three-in-one" capability that is a Petri Net model can be used simultaneously as a graphical representation, a mathematical description, and a simulation tool for the system under study [106]. Therefore, this method has become an accepted technique in mainstream software engineering. One example of the third category is the "Net within Net" model for mobile agent proposed by Köhler and Rölke [78]. This model utilizes the interrelation between a system net and an object net to model four possibilities of a mobile agent object net move, which include spontaneous move, subjective move, objective move and consensual move. Another notable example within the third category is a formal architectural model for logical agent mobility proposed by Xu et. al [179][180]. In this model, a mobile agent system is viewed as a set of agent spaces and agents could migrate from one space to another. Agents are dynamically bound with their environment through an internal connector of an agent space. They use a system net, agent nets, and a connector net to model the environment, agents and the connector respectively. In addition, agent nets are packed up as parts of tokens in system nets. Their model is based on predicate/transition (PrT) nets.

The third method can naturally capture the mobility of a mobile agent inside a mobile agent system and can support formal analysis of several properties of a mobile agent system. It also eliminates the possible errors that occur during the process from modeling to implementation because modeling and simulation of a system happen at the same time. However, our current knowledge shows that security is not supported in the available models within this category.

4.2.4 *Conclusions*

Based on the related works introduced in the previous three sections, we can draw the following conclusions:

1. The security mechanisms used in existing mobile agent systems are either ad-hoc or mainly based on the security features provided by their programming languages such as Java and Safe TCL. Therefore, these existing security mechanisms are usually hard to be generalized and implemented in other programming languages. In addition, most existing mobile agent systems do not have formal methods as their bases. So it is not easy to analyze their features, and verify their security properties and consistency. Meanwhile, those security mechanisms concern more about the mobile agent platform security and do not provide enough investigation to mobile agent security.

2. The related security research work provides wider angles to solve the mobile agent security problems in a mobile agent system from different aspects. However, few of those works is based on formal methods (with exception of SEAL calculus) and little work has been done to provide a generic formal model of a secure mobile agent system.

3. Modeling a mobile agent system is significant and becomes an active topic in the mobile computing area. Among several modeling methods, the one using graphical formal method like Petri Net stands out because of its intuitiveness, effectiveness, and formal treatment of systems and behavioral description. Nevertheless, current Petri Net based mobile agent system models do not take security into their design considerations.

In the next chapter, we will propose an extended Petri Net formalism – Extended Elementary Object System, so that a generic secure mobile agent system model could be based on it.

Chapter 5

A New Formal Model —— Extended Elementary Object System (EEOS)

As a mature formal method, Petri nets are widely used and accepted in the mainstream of software engineering as they are very good formalisms for modeling concurrent systems. They are highly expressive in terms of concurrency, causality, synchronization and non-determinism. They also combine intuitive graphical approaches with a formal definition and description of system structures as well as dynamic behaviors [106]. The intrinsic parallelism and expression power make Petri nets superior to calculus based method [164].

Besides many advantages, Petri Nets are blamed for absence of compositionality. While compositionality is a forte of Object Oriented technology, there have been considerable interests in combining Object Oriented technology with Petri nets in recent years. This is quite natural since both Object Oriented modeling and modeling based on Petri nets aim to support software development by abstraction of objects from the real world and then build a language-independent design using the model which is organized around these objects. And both approaches promote better understanding of requirements, clearer designs and more maintainable systems [161]. The combination of Object Oriented technology and Petri nets equips Petri nets with advantages of Object Oriented technology such as reusability and encapsulation. Petri nets can be easily modified or extended for actual needs or to integrate different mechanisms. Moreover, the encapsulated details of an object will not be affected by the changed parts of its outside world.

63

5.1   Object-Oriented Technology and Petri Nets

According to [182][183], there are three directions to integrate Petri Nets and Object Oriented technology.

The first direction is to integrate Object Oriented concepts into Petri nets. It represents an important trend in the Petri nets community that aims to increase the amount of information held in the tokens in various ways. Tokens of Petri nets in such category represent objects that model the system's static properties, while Petri nets control the overall dynamic behavior of the system. LOOPN [114], SBOPN [111], SimCon [165], Macronet [72], NetCASE [187], OOCPN [87], and OBJSA [90] all belong to this category.

The second direction is to integrate Petri nets into Object Oriented techniques. In this approach, the current marking of the net models the inner state of an object, and transitions in the net may be used to model the execution of method by this object. The approach allows structuring a system by using Object Oriented constructs instead of hierarchical structuring constructs. In addition, this approach allows describing objects with intrinsically concurrent behavior. Using the second category, we often divide a system into several objects and model them individually. Petri nets can also be applied to model the communication mechanisms and protocols between objects. Thus this approach can model both the inner behavior of objects and the inter-objects communications. OBM [69], HOOD nets [45], and PROTOB [7] are representatives of this category.

The third direction is to unify Petri nets and Object Oriented approach. The general idea of this trend is two-folded. Firstly, objects are used to decide the structure of a system to be modeled. Secondly, the behavior of the objects is modeled through Petri nets. In this category, object nets may contain references towards other objects. This approach facilitates modeling multi-layered models with concurrent behaviors. A number of techniques are within this category, such as CO-OPN/2 [13], COOs [9], HOON [93], LOOPN++ [85], OOPN [24], OOPNL [34], OPN [163], and PN-TOX [54]. Among them, OPN has been actively studied. OPN extends the formalism of Coloured Petri nets with a complete integration of Object Oriented features including inheritance, polymorphism and dynamic binding. The Object Orientation provides powerful structuring primitives allowing the modeling of complex systems, including those with multiple levels of activity.

5.2 Elementary Object System (EOS)

The Elementary Object System (EOS) proposed by Valk is an elementary class of OPN [160][161][162][163]. It was originally studied as task system and applied to the modeling of work flow and flexible manufacturing systems [162]. Different from Coloured Petri net, the tokens in an EOS can have the structure of a new Petri net again. To distinguish the two-level Petri nets, the base Petri net holding the special tokens are called *system net* or *environment net*, while the tokens in net form are called *object nets* or *token nets*. An object net can be created, moved or removed in the system net just like an ordinary token, while it has its own structure and can change its markings. The structures of the system net and object nets cannot be changed. EOS does not consider some high level properties of Object Oriented modeling, such as dynamic instantiation, dynamic binding, inheritance, and polymorphism. We choose EOS as the base for our modeling use mainly because: 1) system nets and objects nets in EOS combined together have more powerful modeling capability; 2) the token form of object net can naturally support the modeling of mobility, one of the most important characteristics of a mobile agent system; and 3) EOS leaves room for our security considerations because of its flexible structure. Therefore, we think EOS with certain extensions is appropriate for modeling a generic secure mobile agent system. In the following, we first introduce some basic concepts of EOS.

In an EOS, both the system net and object nets are Elementary Net systems (EN systems). The following definition of EN system appears in [150] in its standard form.

Definition 3.1 An *Elementary Net System* (EN system) $F = (B, E, F, C)$ is defined by a finite set of places (or conditions) B, a finite set of transitions (or events) E, disjoint from F, a flow relation $F \subseteq (B \times E) \cup (E \times B)$, and an initial marking (or initial case) $C \subseteq B$. The occurrence relation for markings C_1, C_2 and a transition t is written as $C_1[t > C_2$ or $C_1 \rightarrow_t C_2$. If t is enabled in C_1, we write $C_1[t >$ or $C_1 \rightarrow_t$. Those notions are extended to words $w \in E^*$ as usual and written as $C_1[w > C_2$ (or $C_1 \rightarrow_w C_2$) and $C_1[w >$ (or $C_1 \rightarrow_w$) respectively. N is called a *structural state machine* if each transition $t \in T$ has exactly one input place ($|\bullet t| = 1$) and exactly one output place ($|t \bullet| = 1$). N is said to be a state machine if it is a structural state machine and C contains exactly one token ($|C| = 1$). $FS(N) := \{w \in E^* \mid C[w >\}$ is the set of *firing* or *occurrence sequences* of N, and $R(N) := \{C_1 \mid \exists w : C_1[w >\}$ is the set of reachable markings or cases, also called the reachability set of N.

Based on the EN system definition, a unary Elementary Object System and related concepts are defined as follows [161].

Definition 3.2 A *unary Elementary Object System* is a tuple $EOS = (SN, ON, \rho)$ where:

$SN = (P, T, W, M_0)$ is an EN system with $|M_0| = 1$, called *system net* of EOS;

$ON = (B, E, F, m_0)$ is an EN system, called object net of EOS, and;

$\rho \subseteq T \times E$ is the interaction relation.

By defining $t\rho := \{e \in E \mid (t, e) \in \rho\}$ and $\rho e := \{t \in T \mid (t, e) \in \rho\}$, it can be derived that there is no element in the interaction relation with t if $t\rho = \phi$.

Definition 3.3 A *bi-marking* of a unary elementary object system $EOS = (SN, ON, \rho)$ is a pair (M, m) where M is a marking of the system net SN and m is a marking of the object net ON.

a) A transition $t \in T$ is activated in a bi-marking (M,m) of EOS if $t\rho = \phi$ and t is activated in M. Then the successor bi-marking (M',m') is defined by $M \xrightarrow{[t,\lambda]} M'$ (w.r.t. SN) and $m = m'$. We write $(M,m) \rightarrow (M',m')$ in this case.

b) A pair $[t,e] \in T \times E$ is activated in a bi-marking (M,m) of EOS if $(t,e) \in \rho$ and both t and e are activated in M and m, respectively. Then the successor bi-marking (M',m') is defined by $M \xrightarrow{[t,e]} M'$ (w.r.t. SN) and $m \rightarrow m'$ (w.r.t. ON). We write $(M,m) \rightarrow (M',m')$ in this case.

c) A transition $e \in E$ is activated in a bi-marking (M,m) of EOS if $\rho e = \phi$ and e is activated in m. Then the successor bi-marking (M',m') is defined by $m \rightarrow m'$ (w.r.t. ON) and $M = M'$. We write $(M,m) \rightarrow (M',m')$ in this case.

Definition 3.3 can be inductively extended to finite sequence $\widetilde{w} \in \Gamma^*$ (where $\Gamma := (T \cup \{\lambda\}) \times (E \cup \{\lambda\}) \setminus [\lambda, \lambda]$) as well for successor bi-marking relation based on a sequence of transitions.

The relation between transitions of the system net and transitions of the object net are called the *interaction relation*. There are three types of interaction relationships in an EOS, namely *interaction, autonomous occurrence*, and *transport*. In transition occurrences of type b) in Definition 3.3, both the system and the object net participate in the same event. Such an occurrence is therefore called an *interaction*. In transition occurrences of type c), the object net changes its state without moving to another place of the system net. It is therefore called *object-autonomous* or *autonomous* for short. The symmetric case in a) is called *system-autonomous* or *transport*, since the object net is transported to a different place without performing an action.

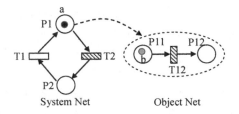

Figure 8 A Simple Example of EOS

Figure 8 shows a simple example of an EOS, in which the dotted circle and dotted arc are only for illustration purposes and do not exist. The system net consists of places P1, P2, transitions T1, T2, and the arcs among them. Token a is an object token whose structure is illustrated by the object net. The object net consists of places P11 and P12, transition T12 and arcs among them. If firing T12 changes the object net marking (for example, token b is moved from P11 to P12) but does not change the system net marking (token a remains in P1 and no other token is generated in the system net), it is called "autonomous occurrence" of T12. If firing T2 changes the system net marking (for example, token a is moved from P1 to P2) but does not change the object net, it is called "transportation". If both system net and object net markings are changed as T2 and T12 are fired simultaneously, it is called "interaction". In this case, the relation between T1 and T12 is called "interaction relation".

5.3   Extended Elementary Object System (EEOS)

5.3.1   *Requirements of a formal method for mobile agent system modeling*

Before we discuss our extensions to the original EOS, it is necessary to consider what the requirements are for a formal method to be used in modeling a generic secure mobile agent system. Our conclusions include the following main aspects:

1) The formal method should be able to naturally and easily capture the mobility of a mobile agent. Since the mobility of a mobile agent is one of the most distinct characteristics of a mobile agent system, the formal method should be able to provide an efficient and convenient mechanism to resemble this characteristic. The mobile agent migration consists of not only a transfer of a mobile agent from one platform to another, but also the entire procedure including: a mobile agent requesting to move, waiting for the current platform's approval, getting processed for a secure transfer after being approved, arriving at the destination platform and being checked and being accepted or denied, etc. Therefore, it is required that the formal method should be capable to model all these details.

2) The formal method can support concurrency and non-determinisms. Generally, a mobile agent system consists of numbers of mobile agent platforms and mobile agents. In the real world, all of these entities can work concurrently. Besides that, their behaviors cannot be determined in advance and vary according to their knowledge, situations or locations. The formal method should be equipped with mechanisms capable to support these features.

3) The formal method can embody object abstraction including encapsulation and information hiding. Abstraction is a basic principle of Object Oriented technology and software architecture, which is the process of extracting the relevant information about a category, entity, or activity, and ignoring the inessential details. An abstraction is an encapsulation that groups a set of related lower-level units of processing and/or structure. An abstraction provides information hiding because it hides inessential details from its users so that they can be ignored. In a generic mobile agent system, both the structural and behavioral details are very complicated. In addition, a mobile agent created by a platform will be executed by another platform. So it is necessary that both the mobile agent and the hosting platform which is not the home platform would not know every detail of the other part for security purposes. Therefore, the proposed formal method should provide an abstraction mechanism to achieve encapsulation and information hiding.

4) The formal method can leave room for security mechanisms design. As discussed in Chapter 2, the security problems are very severe in a mobile agent system and should be given high attention and consideration. To support modeling a secure mobile agent system, the underlining formal method should integrate some mechanisms which support further security design.

The four requirements listed above are the main features that the proposed formal model should have, although they are not intended to be comprehensive.

5.3.2 *Extensions to Elementary Object System*

We extended the original EOS in the following aspects so that it can satisfy the requirements we proposed in the previous section. In the following, these extensions are introduced starting from the simple ones.

5.3.2.1   *Multiple system nets*

In the original Elementary Object System, there is only one system net which can support multiple object nets. A natural way to apply EOS to the mobile agent system is to model mobile agent platforms as system nets and mobile agents as object nets. Since there are multiple mobile agent platforms which may have different structures and utilize various protocols, a single system net in the original EOS is far from being enough for modeling purpose. Multiple system nets can represent multiple categories of platforms. So we extend the original EOS by introducing multiple system nets, each one representing a category of platform.

5.3.2.2   *Multiple layers*

The original EOS only has two layers – system net level and token net level, while the token in a token net cannot be extended. Therefore the modeling capacity is still limited. We extend the semantic by introducing multiple layers. Basically a token net can also be a system net and tokens in it can be token nets in a higher level. This extension enables multi-level encapsulation and embedding; removes the restriction that all system structures and behaviors must be modeled within two layers; and therefore makes the extended EOS more flexible and powerful than the original EOS. The introduction of multiple layers actually necessitates the introduction of multiple system nets in different levels.

5.3.2.3   *Token pool*

In the real world, different relations exist among mobile agent platforms, for example, synchronous and asynchronous communications, exchanging data, and transporting mobile agents among each other. Messages, data, and mobile agents are transferred from one mobile agent platform to the network, and then transferred to another mobile agent platform. Concerning a mobile agent, after it leaves its home platform, probably it has to go through a complex network before it arrives at its destination platform. This network may consist of different computers as nodes, routers, bridges, and other network facilities. In addition, it may utilize various network protocols. We may overlook these network details so as to concentrate more on the migration process between mobile agents and mobile agent platforms, which should be a common procedure in a generic mobile agent system. "Token Pool" is introduced for this purpose.

Token pool is a special place in an extended EOS. There is only one token pool in an EEOS model, which connects to each system net in the base layer as both an input and output place. In addition, autonomous occurrence of the transitions of token nets (which will be used to represent mobile agents in the generic mobile agent system model) cannot happen in the token pool. This extension introduces a concept of "center" into the EEOS model mainly from the logical perspective while each token net needs to go through this center. Even if the "center" is very complicated and large, it is still considered as a whole in the base level and its details are invisible to each system net. This extension leaves space for the communications and coordination modeling among different components of this "center" and between this "center" and system nets representing mobile agent platforms. Meanwhile, it also leaves room for security design during token nets migration. Different tokens, which could be messages, data or mobile agents, are moved from one system net to the token pool once they leave the platform, and then from the token pool to another system net. Token pool has its own structure as well. Based on needs, such structure can reflect the network connections to some extent, or even include more details about the entity in the network which connects those system nets together, such as a router. Token pool and system nets combined together form the system nets level in our EEOS. Figure 9 illustrates the star connection between a token pool with system nets.

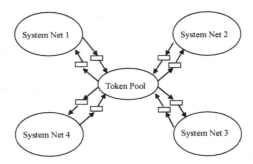

Figure 9 Star Connection between Token Pool and System Nets

5.3.2.4   *Internal places, external places and internal transitions, external transitions*

In an ordinary EOS, there is no difference between places in the sense that they are holders of tokens and also no difference between transitions in the sense that their firing may change markings of places. To enhance EEOS support for security and object orientation, we introduce the concepts of internal/external places and internal/connection transitions into our EEOS.

In an EEOS, an *internal place* is a place which can only be seen and accessed by the net which semantically includes this place (this net is called the *home net* for that place). An *external place* is a place which can be seen and accessed by nets other than the home net of that place. The markings of external places can be read or changed by the outside world as well as its home net. An *internal transition* is only connected to places of its home net and cannot be accessed outside of its home net. An *external transition* can connect to the external places of nets other than its home net. External places and external transitions are used to connect different nets together. If a net is viewed as an object, its internal places are like the private data members which are only known by this object; its internal transitions are like the private member functions which can operate on the private data members of this object; its external places are like the public data members which can be read or written freely by other objects; and its external transitions are like public member functions which can be called by other objects. For simplicity, we don't consider protected data members or member functions here. A *test arc* connecting a place and a transition can make sure that when this transition is fired, the marking of the place is not changed.

Figure 10 illustrates a simple example for two nets (Net A and Net B) connected to each other. We use single circle (such as Pa3 in Net A) for internal place, concentric circle (such as Pa2) for external place, shaded rectangle (Ta1) for internal transition, and clear rectangle (Ta4) for external transition. Test arc is represented by an arc with a solid circle at the end to transition.

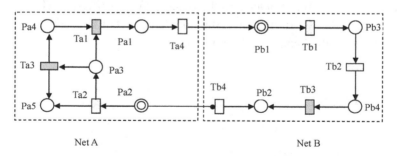

Net A   Net B

Figure 10 Internal/External Places and Internal/Connection Transitions

By restricting the visibility and accessibility of places and transitions, we can guarantee that the markings of internal places of a net should only be changed by firing some transitions of this net. Nets interact with each other through their external places and external transitions. Usually we can use external places/transitions of a net, which act as interfaces of an object, for communication purposes. This extension endows the EEOS with better capability for object abstraction, information hiding and encapsulation, which are critical for security design.

5.3.2.5   *Two new arcs*

A simple and expressive model is beneficial for understanding it. Therefore, we introduce two new arcs into our EEOS to simplify the model and support characteristics such as non-determinism of a mobile agent system.

The first one is the *update arc*, which describes the change of marking in a place when some transition connected to that place fires. This arc carries a hollow arrow tip at one end (to place) and a solid arrow tip at the other end (to transition). When a transition linked to such an update arc is fired, some token(s) is(are) removed from the place at the other end of the arc, and at the same time some token(s) is(are) added to the same place as well. The token(s) removed from the place and the token(s) added to the place may be different. They can be the same certainly. In that case, the update arc acts like a test arc. Figure 11 illustrates the behavior of an update arc.

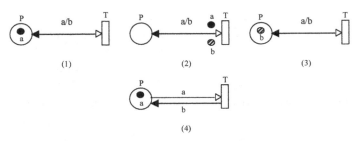

Figure 11 Update Arc

In Figure 11, (1) is before firing of transition T, (2) is during the firing of transition T, and (3) is after the firing. (4) shows the equivalent EOS for (1). The firing rule of the update arc is as follows: $M'(P) = M(P) - a + b$. By introducing the update arc, we can save an extra arc to model the same behavior of a mobile agent system, thus simplifying the entire model and simulation process.

Another arc we introduce is differ-remove arc, which actually consists of two arcs starting from the same place and ending at two different transitions. One end carries a hollow arrow tip; the other carries a solid arrow tip. This arc is introduced to deal with different actions of some transition in different situations. Recall that in an Object Petri Net each component is an object. We can abstract an object transition from some transitions with similar semantics; therefore simplify the modeling of some behaviors with same or similar semantics. The new arc is shown in Figure 12 (1) and its equivalent EOS is shown in Figure 12 (2).

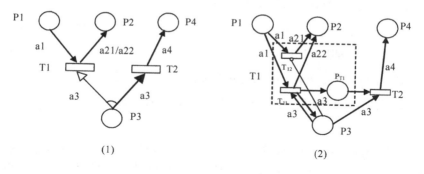

(1)   (2)

Figure 12 Differ-remove Arc

From (2) we can see that the firing of T1 is different according to the token color in place P3. There is an inhibitor arc connecting place P3 and sub transition T_{12} with label a3. So when P3 only holds token(s) with color other than a3, sub transition T_{12} is possible to fire. When place P1 holds token(s) with color a1, transition T_{12} is enabled. The firing result would be the removal of token a1 from P1 and generation of token with color a21 in place P2. In this case, token(s) in place P3 does not (do not) participate in the firing. So we call this kind of firing "*non-participation firing*". The situation is different when place P3 holds token(s) with color a3. The existence of the inhibitor arc inhibits the firing of T_{12}. But if place P1 holds token(s) with color a1, sub transition T_{11} would become enabled. Therefore it can be fired and the result would be removal of token a1 from P1, generation of token a22 into place P2, reservation of token a3 in P3 (the arc from place P3 to T1 is like a reservation arc in this aspect) and generation of a special token "enabled" to place P_{T1}. Successively, T2 is enabled and can fire with the result that token a3 and the special token are removed from their places and generation a token with color a4 in P4. In this case, the token in P3 participates in the firing of T1, therefore we call it "*participation firing*".

The firing rules for both firing modes are described as follows.

1) For non-participation firing

$$M'(P1) = M(P1) - a1, M'(P2) = M(P2) + a21,$$
$$M'(P3) = M(P3), M'(P4) = M(P4)$$

2) For participation firing.

$$M'(P1) = M(P1) - a1, M'(P2) = M(P2) + a22,$$
$$M'(P3) = M(P3) - a3, M'(P4) = M(P4) + a4$$

.

The introduction of the differ-remove arc helps us simplify the model and meanwhile supports one of the characteristics of a mobile system that is non-determinism. One case for non-determination is that a different behavior is performed for the same action when the knowledge of a mobile agent or the message it receives is different. For example, with respect to agent migration, a mobile agent can decide when and where it should go and initiate the migration, which is called an "active migration"; while a mobile agent platform can decide when and where the mobile agent should go and request the mobile agent to migrate, the migration in the latter case is called a "passive migration".

5.3.2.6   *Extended interaction relation*

In our EEOS, extended interaction relation is still between a pair of transitions in a system net and an object net, say T1 and T2. Different from the original interaction relation, extended interaction relation allows one transition, say T1, to be fired right before the firing of the other transition T2. The firing of T1 and the extended interaction relation between T1 and T2 are the additional conditions for firing T2. In other words, if T2 is enabled, it won't be fired until T1 fires, and it should be fired right after T1 fires. We call T1 as *"driving transition"* and T2 as *"driven transition"*. Figure 13 illustrates this relation. Formally speaking, suppose *EIR(T1, T2)* stand for the extended interaction relation between T1 and T2, *Fire(T, t)* mean transition T fires at time point t, *Enable(T,t)* mean transition T is enabled at time point t, then we have:

$$EIR(T1, T2) \Leftrightarrow (Fire(T1, t) \land Enable(T2, t) \Rightarrow Fire(T1, t + \varepsilon)\, (\varepsilon \to 0)).$$

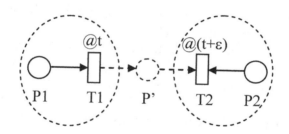

Figure 13 Extended Interaction Relation

Extending the interaction relation leaves room for modeling a more complex relationship between a system net and an object net. It also enables us to design certain security mechanism to a mobile agent system. The detailed timing handling is beyond the scope of this thesis and belongs to our future consideration.

5.3.3 *Formal specification of Extended Elementary Object System*

The formal specification of Extended Elementary Object System (EEOS) is presented as follows.

Definition 3.3 Extended Elementary Object System (EEOS) An EEOS is a tuple $EEOS = (SN, ON, \rho, \tau)$ where

1. $SN = (SN_1, SN_2, \cdots, SN_i, \cdots, SN_n, TP)$ is the set of system nets $SN_i (i = 1, \cdots, n)$ and the token pool TP. Each system net SN_i is a tuple $SN_i = (SID_i, P_i, T_i, F_i, K_i, W_i, M_{0i})$ where

   (1) SID_i is a unique identifier of the system net;

   (2) P_i is a finite set of places $P_{ij} (j = 1, \cdots, J)$;

   (3) T_i is a finite set of transitions $T_{ir} (r = 1, \cdots, R)$;

   (4) F_i is a finite set of directed arcs $F_{ih} (h = 1, \cdots, H)$ between places and transitions;

   (5) K_i is a set of tokens with colors or referencing to object nets $K_{ic} (c = 1, \cdots, C)$;

   (6) W_i is a set of label function $W_{ih} (h = 1, \cdots, H)$ which assign expressions to arcs $F_{ih} (h = 1, \cdots, H)$;

   (7) M_{0i} is the initial marking of SN_i, which lists the token(s) held in each place of SN_i in the form of $(m_{o\_P_{i1}}, m_{o\_P_{i2}}, \cdots, m_{o\_P_{ij}}, \cdots m_{o\_P_{iJ}})$ where $m_{o\_P_{ij}}$ is a multiset of K_i.

   TP is a place which connects with each system net SN_i. There is only one TP in each EEOS.

2. $ON = (ON_1, ON_2, \cdots, ON_l, \cdots, ON_m)$ is the set of m object nets $ON_l (l = 1, \cdots, m)$, which can again be a system net but without the token pool for higher level object nets. Each object net is a tuple $ON_l = (OID_l, P_l, T_l, F_l, K_l, W_l, M_{0l})$ in which symbols have similar meanings to those above. OID_l is the unique identifier of this object net; P_l is the place set; T_l is the transition set; F_l is the arc set; K_l are the token set; W_l is the label functions set associated with F_l; and M_{0l} is the initial marking of ON_l.

3. ρ is the set of extended interaction relations $\rho \subseteq \bigcup f_{ab} : T_a \times T_b$ between transitions set T_a in system net SN_a and transitions set T_b in object net ON_b . Suppose $EIR(T_1, T_2)$ stands for the extended interaction relationship between transitions T_1 and T_2 . We have $f_{ab} \subseteq \bigcup (EIR(T_{ar}, T_{br'}) \vee EIR(T_{br'}, T_{ar}))$ where $T_{ar} \in T_a$ and $T_{br'} \in T_b$.

4. τ is the set of referencing functions $\tau \subseteq \bigcup mf_x : K_x \times ON$ from tokens set K_x in system net SN_x to object nets ON . Each $mf_x \subseteq \bigcup mf_{xy}(K_{xy}, ON_{y'})$ where $K_{xy} \in K_x$ and $ON_{y'} \in ON$.

Definition 3.4 ($|ITi|$ is the set of internal transitions of net i and $|ETi|$ is the set of external transitions of net i.)

1. An *internal place* InP of a net is a place such that $(\bullet InP) \cup (InP\bullet) \subseteq |IT_i| \cup |ET_i|$.

2. An *external place* ExP of a net is a place such that $((\bullet ExP) \cup (ExP\bullet) \subseteq |IT_i| \cup |ET_j|) \wedge \neg ((\bullet ExP) \cup (ExP\bullet) \subseteq |IT_i|)$.

Definition 3.5 A **bi-marking** of an extended elementary object system is a pair (M, m) where $M = (M_1, ..., M_i, ..., M_n, M_{TP})$ is a marking of SN and token pool, and $m = (m_1, ..., m_i, ..., m_{n'})$ is a marking of ON .

1. A transition $t \in T_i$ is activated in a bi-marking (M, m) of EEOS if $\neg EIR(e, t)$ where $e \in T_j'$ and t is activated in $_t$ M . Then the successor bi-marking (M', m') is defined by $M \rightarrow M'$ (w.r.t. SN) and $m = m'$. We write $(M, m) \rightarrow (M', m')$ in this case.

2. A transition $e \in T_j'$ is activated in a bi-marking (M, m) of EOS if $\neg EIR(t, e)$ where $t \in T_i$ and e is activated in m . Then the successor bi-marking (M', m') is defined by $m \rightarrow m'$ (w.r.t. ON) and $M = M'$. We write $(M, m) \rightarrow (M', m')$ in this case.

3. A pair $[t, e] \in T \times E$ is activated in a bi-marking (M, m) of EOS if $EIR(t, e) \vee EIR(e, t)$, t and e are activated in M and m respectively. Then the successor bi-marking (M', m') is defined by $M \rightarrow M'_{[t,e]}$ (w.r.t. SN) and $m \rightarrow m'$ (w.r.t. ON). We write $(M, m) \rightarrow (M', m')$ in this case.

Chapter 6

A Formal Framework of a Generic Secure Mobile Agent System Based on EEOS

In this chapter, we propose a formal framework of a generic secure mobile agent system based on the Extended Elementary Object System (EEOS) we proposed in Chapter 3. This framework includes a hierarchical structure of a mobile agent system, supports dynamic connection and communication between mobile agents and their mobile agent platforms, supports both weak and strong mobility of mobile agents, and also integrates a model of security mechanisms for mobile agent platforms as well as mobile agents during mobile agent migration and execution. We will discuss four aspects: structure, communication, mobility and security in the following.

6.1 Structure of a Mobile Agent System

The generic mobile agent system we considered contains several mobile agent platforms and mobile agents. A mobile agent platform is able to create and dispatch different mobile agents, receives, executes or refuses to execute mobile agents of its own or from other platforms, and delete mobile agents when necessary. Its computation resources are under control to avoid possible attacks from malicious mobile agents. A mobile agent has its own structure, knowledge, goals and is equipped with different security mechanisms. Some part of those security mechanisms are integrated into the structure of a mobile agent for security routine such as authentication. Other parts are independent from the structure so that different security mechanisms can be applied to the generic system dynamically and conveniently as long as their interfaces comply with the principles predefined. Therefore in our model, a mobile agent system can be abstracted into three layers: mobile agent platform layer, mobile agent layer and security mechanism layer. Platform layer is the base layer and consists of several mobile agent platforms, modeled as system nets, and the token pool. In this layer, mobile agents are tokens that can be transported among system nets via the token pool. The detailed structure and behaviors of a mobile agent are modeled in the second layer, i.e. mobile agent layer. In this layer, mobile agents are system nets while the security mechanisms equipped with mobile agents are tokens. It should also be noted that a mobile agent platform should also be equipped with certain security mechanisms in the platform layer. The structure of the security mechanisms is modeled in the top layer, security mechanism layer. Figure 14 illustrates the hierarchy model of a generic secure mobile agent system (MAS).

Our mobile agent system model is abstracted into three layers. Figure 14 illustrates a high-level hierarchical EEOS model for a generic secure mobile agent system. The mobile agent platform layer is the base layer abd consists of n platforms modeled as system nets and the token pool. In this layer, mobile agents are tokens that can be transported among system nets via the token pool. The structures and behaviors of mobile agents are modeled in the mobile agent layer. In this layer, mobile agents are system nets while the security mechanisms equipped with mobile agents are tokens. The security mechanisms are modeled in the top layer, security mechanism layer.

Before the detailed discussions, we introduce the assumptions for our system. First of all, our model is targeted for application software, which is running on a generic operating system (OS). Therefore, all components of the model can only utilize the OS utilities, but cannot change them. For example, a platform cannot change the way the OS runs the executables to achieve its goal. Secondly, the OS is equipped with certain protocols protecting messages against replay attack, such as

IPSec protocol running on Windows 2000. In addition, similar protocols could be integrated with our model so that our model does not need to take replay attack into consideration.

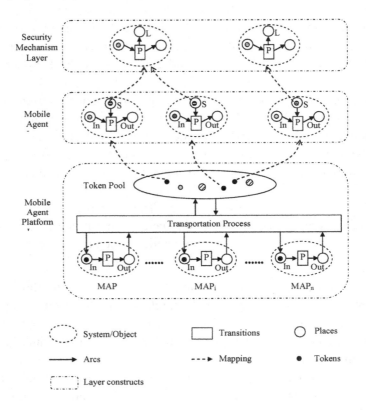

Figure 14 High-level Hierarchical Model for a Generic Secure Mobile Agent System

6.1.1 *Mobile agent platform*

The bottom layer of a mobile agent system is the mobile agent platform layer, which is the system net layer for its upper layer mobile agent object nets. It consists of two components: mobile agent platforms and the trust server residing in the token pool. In this section , mobile agent platform is to be discussed. Its functionalities and components will be summarized first, which is followed by its EEOS model. Afterwards its various functionalities will be introduced in more details. The trust server will be discussed in section 6.1.2.

6.1.1.1 *Functionalities and components of a mobile agent platform*

As we discussed before, a mobile agent platform is responsible for managing, transporting and executing mobile agents in their life spans. A mobile agent platform not only communicates with mobile or static agents residing on it through its internal communication channels, but also communicates with other platforms or third parties through its external communication channels. Figure 15 shows the functionality parties of a mobile agent platform.

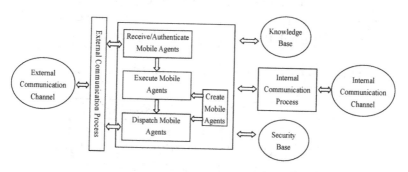

Figure 15 Functionality Parts of a Mobile Agent Platform

As shown in Figure 15, a mobile agent platform receives a mobile agent through the external communication channel as mobile agents always come to a mobile agent platform from the trust server in the token pool. Then the mobile agent platform authenticates the identity of this mobile agent based on its own knowledge base and security base. At the same time, the mobile agent platform also needs to prove its identity to the incoming mobile agent to achieve mutual authentication. The latter part requires the platform to send its identity to the mobile agent through its internal communication channel. Only after the mutual authentication is succeeded can the mobile agent platform go ahead to execute the mobile agent. For secure mobile agent execution for both mobile agent platform and mobile agent, the execution can only occur under certain security mechanisms and in specific places of a mobile agent platform for security monitoring. During this process, the mobile agent platform and mobile agent communicate with each other. After the execution is over, the mobile agent platform will send the mobile agent to the token pool again so that it can go to other platforms or return to its home platform from there. Although this procedure is sequential for one mobile agent, since a mobile agent platform can support multiple mobile agents simultaneously, such managing of multiple mobile agents is concurrent and parallel.

Besides being responsible for the management of incoming mobile agents from other platforms, a mobile agent platform is also capable of creating its own mobile agents. It may execute its own mobile agents first, then dispatch them to the network at the mobile agents' will or at its own will or dispatch them directly after they are created.

6.1.1.2 *EEOS model of a mobile agent platform*

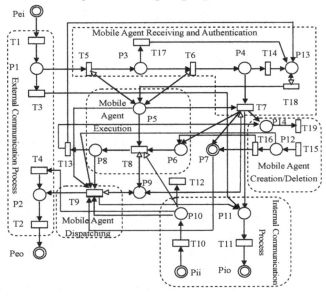

Figure 16 Simplified EEOS Model of a Mobile Agent Platform

In our EEOS model, a mobile agent platform consists of six functionality components, which include external and internal communication process, mobile agent receiving and authentication, mobile agent execution, mobile agent dispatching and mobile agent creation, as illustrated in Figure 16. Due to space limitation, Figure 16 cannot show all the details such as different dispatching methods for active migration and passive migration, which will be introduced later in section 6.2.2. Table 1 is the legend for Figure 16.

Places	Meaning	Transitions	Functions
Pei	Externally incoming communication channels	T1	Process externally incoming communications
Peo	Externally outgoing communication channels	T2	Process externally outgoing communications
Pii	Internally incoming/outgoing communication channels	T3	Process externally incoming info and forward to internal agents
Pio	Internally outgoing communication channels	T4	Process internally incoming info and forward to outside world
P1	Incoming info/MAs	T5	Decrypt a MA using its private key
P2	Outgoing info/MAs	T6	Authenticate a MA (identifier pair check)
P3	Holder for MAs after authentication process	T7	Deliver MA to ready queue and info to internally outgoing channel
P4	Holder for MAs after identifiers check	T8	Execute MAs
P5	Security base	T9	Dispatch MAs
P6	Holder for MAs ready for execution	T10	Process internally incoming info
P7	Record MAs on this platform	T11	Process internally outgoing info
P8	Holder for MAs after execution	T12	Differ-remove arc transition
P9	Knowledge base	T13	Send malicious MAs to

			Prison
P10	Holder for processed internal incoming communication info	T14	Send suspected malicious MAs to Prison
P11	Holder for internal outgoing communication info	T15	Create MAs
P12	Holder for self-created MAs	T16	Put self-created MAs to ready queue
P13	Prison for malicious MAs	T17	Send unauthenticated MA to Prison
P14	Holder for MAs to be deleted	T18	Record malicious MAs/MAPs info to Security Base
		T19	Delete MAs

Table 1 Legend for Figure 16

In the simplified EEOS model for a mobile agent platform, there are four external places: Pei (external input), Peo (external output), Pii (internal input), and Pio (internal output). Pei and Peo form the external communication channels which are not only for transporting mobile agents, but also for exchanging messages, information and data with other platforms, trust server or third parties. Pii and Pio form the internal communication channels which are used for communications between this mobile agent platform and mobile agents or static agents residing on it. We want to mention that place P7, which is used to record mobile agents residing on this platform, is an external place. That is to achieve the dynamic connection between the mobile agent platform and mobile agents. Since EEOS does not support changing of structure, we choose to implement a complete connection and dynamically enable certain transitions to control the direction of actual communications. Therefore, recording mobile agents on mobile agent platforms are of importance to the realization of dynamic communication. We will spread the discussion about this aspect in section 6.2. Other functionality components are presented in the following sections.

6.1.1.2.1   *Create and delete mobile agent*

Generally speaking, a mobile agent platform should have templates for mobile agents that it can create. When a mobile agent platform creates a mobile agent, it instantiates an instance of the corresponding template. One of the main aspects of this instantiation is to assign a unique identifier header to the mobile agent. To do this, the platform sends a request to the trust server (which will be discussed in Section 6.1.2). In the request message, the platform has to encrypt its unique identifier (also assigned by the trust server) by its private key and the trust server's public key, and then sends the message to the trust server. The trust server decrypts the message and checks its mobile agent registration table, then assign a unique identifier pair in the form of *(HPI, SI)* where *HPI* represents the home platform identifier and *SI* represents the self identifier of the mobile agent to be created. Afterwards, the trust server encrypts this header using its private key and the public key of the platform, and sends it back. The platform decrypts the message, gets the identifier header, and attaches it to the mobile agent token. This header can only be written once and is bounded to the mobile agent token all the time through its life span. In the real application, the "one-time write" feature can be supported by certain data type in programming languages, such as "static const" in C++. Another aspect of the instantiation is to correlate the mobile agent token net with the platform system net. It is achieved through depositing "critical tokens". Figure 17 illustrates a simplified example. Firing T0 in the system net will put token "a" into place P1, which represents that a mobile agent "a" is generated. At the same time, a token "c" is put into place P10 in the object net which enables the activities of the object net. These two aspects combined together represent the mobile agent creation and activation. Here, token "a" and "c" are called "critical tokens".

When a mobile agent platform is going to delete a mobile agent, it withdraws the critical tokens simultaneously. Similarly, a child mobile agent spawn from and absorbed by an existing mobile agent can also be modeled by putting and removing critical tokens to/from corresponding mobile agent nets. Agent cloning is not considered here. But our EEOS has the capacity to model agent cloning. In addition, the mobile agent platform will have to inform the trust server of the identifier of the mobile agent it deletes.

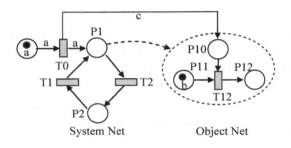

Figure 17 Create a Mobile Agent

6.1.1.2.2   *Transport and register mobile agent*

Transporting mobile agents includes dispatching and receiving mobile agents through the external communication channels of platforms. There are three ways to dispatch a mobile agent. First, the mobile agent proposes to leave the current platform by itself. Second, the mobile agent will be asked to move by the hosting platform. In this case, the platform determines when and where the mobile agent should go. Third, the mobile agent is called by another platform. Therefore, the abstract transition T9 in Figure 16 can be refined for these three situations. No matter which way the mobile agent is going to be dispatched, the hosting platform needs to prepare the outgoing mobile agent by going through a procedure, which includes a two-round encryption. Similarly, when a mobile agent platform receives an incoming mobile agent, it also needs to process the mobile agent following another decryption procedure to verify the identity of the mobile agent. Theses procedures will be discussed in detail in section 6.3. To make the next chapter trust server easy to understand, we briefly summarize the procedure of dispatching a mobile agent.

A mobile agent platform first encrypts the mobile agent with its unique identifier header by using the private key of this platform. Afterwards, it appends the destination platform, the path history and the unique identifier header of this mobile agent to the encrypted mobile agent. Then it encrypts the newly-packed mobile agent using the public key of the trusted server. Figure 18 illustrates the mobile agent being packed and encrypted. Finally, the encrypted packed mobile agent is put into a queue of out-going mobile agents on this platform and will be dispatched when the platform and the network are both ready.

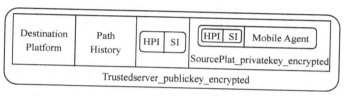

Figure 18 Packed and Encrypted Mobile Agent

Registration of a mobile agent happens after an incoming mobile agent has been authenticated. The hosting platform checks the identifiers header *(HPI, SI)* of that mobile agent in its "dangerous-entity list", which is built and updated on the fly and contains records in the form of $< plat\_ID, ma\_ID, info >$ with *info* records malicious action information. If the header is found, the platform may refuse this mobile agent and freeze it in prison P12, or kill it directly according to the *info* content and its policies. If not, the platform assumes this mobile agent is benign and puts it into place P6 for execution. At the same time, the platform updates a "registration table" in its security base accordingly, which records the mobile agents having visited it and is illustrated in Table 2. In this table, the identifiers pairs of mobile agents, their source platforms, and their arrival and departure times are to be kept. The destination platform inserts a new entry into this table for each incoming mobile agent which passes mutual authentication. If a mobile agent has done any malicious deed during its execution, besides corresponding punishment, a new record will be added to the dangerous-entity list of the hosting platform accordingly for future check. The trust level and role will be introduced in section 6.4.3.2.

(Home Platform Identifier, Mobile Agent Identifier)	Source Platform Identifier	Arrival Time	Departure Time	Trust Level	Role

Table 2 Registration Table for Incoming Mobile Agents on a Mobile Agent Platform

Once the registration process is accomplished, this incoming mobile agent can be executed. The "execution" transition will be discussed further in section 6.1.1.2.3. After the execution is terminated by the mobile agent platform on detection of any malicious action, or after a successful execution, the mobile agent will be put into place P8. For the former situation, this mobile agent will be put into the prison. Once a new mobile agent is put into prison, the mobile agent platform records its identifier and its home platform's identifier into a list indicating malicious agents. Then the platform can go ahead and deal with it, such as denying its services and sending it away, or directly freezing it, or even eliminating it. For the latter situation, this mobile agent will be dispatched to the outside world under different policies depending on whether the mobile agent requests to move itself, or the outside world requests it, or the mobile agent platform wants it to leave. But for a secure transfer, the mobile agent platform will always encrypt the mobile agent using its own private key; append the identifiers of the destination platform and of itself as the source destination platform, together with the original identifier pair of this mobile agent to the encrypted mobile agent then encrypt the whole again using the public key of the trusted server and afterwards send the encrypted mobile agent to the network. Due to the limited space, those policies are not illustrated in Figure 16.

It should be noted that the unique identifier header of a mobile agent cannot be changed after it is created. And it is the trust server that assigns the header. Even if a malicious platform may attempt to change the header appended to the mobile agent when it dispatches the mobile agent, the trust server, which the mobile agent must visit before arriving at another platform, checks it and makes sure only mobile agents with a correct header can go through. This is the base for the mobile agent registration.

6.1.1.2.3   *Execute mobile agent*

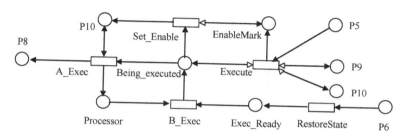

Figure 19 Mobile Agent Execution

Execution of a mobile agent, which is represented by T8 in Figure 16 is refined in Figure 19. After a mobile agent is put into the ready queue P6, its state is restored if strong mobility is to be achieved, which will be discussed in section 6.3.1. Next when a processor is available, the mobile agent acquires the processor and executes in the place "Being_executed". It remains in that place during the whole execution process so a mobile agent platform can reinforce its security by applying certain mechanism to place "Being_executed", like the "sandbox". In this way, a platform can fully monitor the execution of a mobile agent. During its execution, information from the Knowledge Base of the platform (P9) and communication between the platform and the mobile agent (P11) may be needed. If during the execution this mobile agent is found doing malicious stuff, it will be forced to give up the execution and processor and placed to P8, then moved to the prison. Meanwhile, the platform records the corresponding home platform identifier and the malicious mobile agent's identifier into its dangerous-party list for future reference. After the mobile agent accomplishes its tasks, it releases the processor and is placed to P8. Different processor scheduling methods may be used in real world applications and are out of our considerations in this thesis. Based on what have been discussed, a list of behaviors of a mobile agent platform supported by our EEOS model can be identified below, which are illustrated by Figure 16 and Table 1. We used the following notations:

Notation	Meaning
$P1(+P2) \rightarrow T1$	$*T1 = \{P1, P2\}$
$T1 \mid T2 \rightarrow P1$	$*P1 = \{T1, T2\}$
$T1 \rightarrow P1 \mid P2$	$T1* = \{P1, P2\}$
$P1[+P2] \rightarrow T1[+T2]$	There is a differ-remove arc between place $P2$ and transitions $T1, T2$.

Table 3 Notations

1. Receive, authenticate, and check a mobile agent:
   $Pei \rightarrow T1 \rightarrow P1(+P5) \rightarrow T5 \rightarrow P3(+P5) \rightarrow T6 \rightarrow P4$
2. Authenticate itself to a mobile agent:
   $P4 \rightarrow T7 \rightarrow P11(+P6+P7) \rightarrow T11 \rightarrow Pio$
3. Execute a mobile agent: $P6(+P9+P10+P5) \rightarrow T8 \rightarrow P8$
4. Dispatch a mobile agent:
   $P8(+P5+P12+P10+P7+P9) \rightarrow T9 \rightarrow P2 \rightarrow T2 \rightarrow Peo$
5. External message incoming: $Pei \rightarrow T1 \rightarrow P1 \rightarrow T3$
6. External message outgoing: $T1[+T9] \rightarrow P2 \rightarrow T2 \rightarrow Peo$
7. Internal message incoming: $Pii \rightarrow T10 \rightarrow P10$
8. Internal message outgoing: $P11 \rightarrow T11 \rightarrow Pio$

6.1.2   *Trust server*

To ensure that a mobile agent transfer is secure and reinforce non-repudiation, we introduce a trust server (abbreviated as TS in the following) into the framework of a generic mobile agent system. The TS is located in the token pool in our EEOS model. The token pool is a conceptual place in an EEOS model to represent the common processing of a mobile agent during its migration. A simplified view of the trust server is illustrated in Figure 20 and its legend is in Table 4.

Normally, the TS performs the following three steps after a mobile agent arrives: identifies the mobile agent; checks and registers the mobile agent; and dispatches the mobile agent.

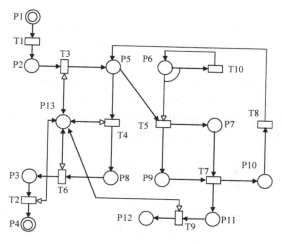

Figure 20 EEOS Model for the Trust Server in the Token Pool

Places	Meaning	Transitions	Functions
P1, P2, P3, P4	In communication channel Out communication channel	T1,T2	Process in/out communications
P5	Incoming mobile agent holder	T3	Decrypt the incoming mobile agent
P6	Trust model holder	T4	Register/Check registration of mobile agent
P7	Original mobile agent identifier holder	T5	Decrypt the mobile agent using claimed source platform public key
P8	Outgoing mobile agent holder	T6	Encrypt the outgoing mobile agent
P9	Original encrypted mobile agent holder	T7	Compare the mobile agent identifier header
P10	Trusted mobile agent holder	T8	Send trusted mobile agent for registration
P11	Bad mobile agent holder	T9	Update security base

P12	Bad mobile agent holder		T10	Differ-remove transition	arc

Table 4 Legend for Figure 20

As it is a requirement that a mobile agent platform should encrypt an outgoing mobile agent using the trust server's public key in the end as introduced in section 6.1.1.2.2, the trust server firstly decrypts an incoming mobile agent using its private key stored in its security base P13. Transaction T3 in Figure 20 represents the decryption. Afterwards, the TS knows the destination platform, the current path history and the identifier header (HPI, SI) of this mobile agent.

MA-IdPair	Dest-PlatId	Sour-PlatId	A-Time	D-Time	P-History
(MAP1, MA1)	MAP2	MAP1	14:00 04/15/2004	14:02 04/15/2004	[[1, MAP1, 12:30:04/15/2004]]
(MAP2, MA10)	MAP1	MAP3	16:30 04/15/2004	16:40 04/15/2004	[[1, MAP2, 15:20:04/15/2004] [2, MAP3, 16:00:04/15/2004]]
••••••	••••••	••••••	••••••	••••••	••••••

Table 5 Mobile Agents Table Maintained by the Trust server

Secondly, the TS checks whether this mobile agent has already been transferred to it before and registers the mobile agent accordingly. This process is represented by the transition T4. The TS maintains a table of mobile agents in its security base P13. In this table, each mobile agent ever being transferred in this system has one entry. The table has six fields, including mobile agent identifier header (MA-IdPair), destination platform identifier (Dest-PlatId), source platform identifier (Sour-PlatId), arriving time (A-Time), departure time (D-Time), and path history (P-History). It should be noted that the source platform is the one which sends the mobile agent to the TS and not necessarily the home platform of a mobile agent. The data type of P-History field is a list which can only be appended at the end. Each element of the list is of the type [Visit#, Platform-Id, Visit-Time] , which means at "Visit-Time" this mobile agent visits the "Visit#"th platform indicated by "Platform-Id". The schema and some sample data entries of this mobile agents table is shown in Table 5.

Since each mobile agent is uniquely identified by its identifier header, the TS only needs to check the identifier pair to see whether it is already in the table. If it is not, the TS will insert a new entry for this mobile agent into the above table and record all fields. It will copy the identifier pair, the destination platform identifier, and its path history directly to the MA-IdPair, Dest-PlatId, and P-History fields respectively. Since this mobile agent must have just left its home platform, the TS records its home platform as its Sour-PlatId. Corresponding arrival time is recorded into A-Time field and departure time is temporarily left blank in the D-Time field. On the contrary, if the identifier header of a mobile agent has already been in the mobile agents table, the TS will perform a sequence of actions to check the mobile agent before it updates the corresponding entry for this mobile agent. The TS first checks the Dest_PlatId in the current entry for the mobile agent with the latest path history (in the form of [Visit#, Platform-Id, Visit-Time]) it got from the mobile agent. The Dest_PlatId and Platform-Id are supposed to match. Then the TS checks the Visit-Time field in the latest path history it got from the mobile agent with both the arrival time of the mobile agent and the Visit-Time field of the last element of the current P-History. It is assumed that the whole mobile agent system uses the same timing system. If a mobile agent comes to the TS from a platform which is in a different time zone from that of the TS, the time will be adjusted accordingly before this check. The former Visit-Time value is supposed to be between the arrival time and the latter Visit-Time value. If so, the TS inserts the new path history as the last element to the current P-History, updates Sour-PlatId to the Platform-Id value in the new path history, records the Dest-PlatId, A-Time and also leaves the D-Time blank. It should be noted that the TS will reset the path-list of a mobile agent to NIL (empty list) after it records the path in the mobile agents table. The purpose of this process is two-folded. On the one hand, the size of a mobile agent continuing its traveling gets smaller, which creates less traffic and faster migration. On the other hand, a potential malicious mobile agent platform will have no way to perform attacks against the mobile agent path history. If a mobile agent platform wants the path history of a certain mobile agent, it can ask the TS for it while the TS can decide whether such request should be serviced according to certain policies. Except for the path list, the TS does not change any other information carried by the mobile agent. Afterwards, the TS will put the mobile agent into the queue for out-going mobile agents represented by place P8 for dispatching.

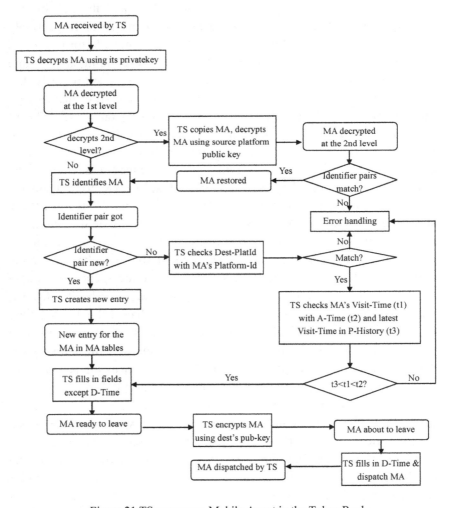

Figure 21 TS accesses a Mobile Agent in the Token Pool

Thirdly, the TS will dispatch the mobile agent to its destination platform. The TS encrypts (T6) the packed mobile agent using the public key of the destination platform stored in P13, and then puts the encrypted mobile agent to place P3, from where the mobile agent will go to the destination platform. At the same time, the TS records the departure time of this mobile agent into the D-Time field in the corresponding entry in the mobile agents table.

The three steps are normally performed by the TS for any incoming mobile agent. We can see that most of the actions are based on the checking of the identifier header carried by a mobile agent. How about if the identifier header (HPI, SI) was modified by a malicious mobile agent platform and appended to the original mobile agent?

To prevent misidentifying the mobile agent caused by such modification, the TS can select to perform another decryption (T5) using the public key of the source platform of the mobile agent. Then TS can get the original identifier header (stored in place P7). Before this decryption, TS should make a copy of the original encrypted mobile agent using the private key of this agent's source platform in P9. Since the original identifier header is read-only whose value can only be assigned once when this mobile agent is created, any platform the mobile agent visits does not have the ability to change its value. Therefore, the TS can compare (T7) the original identifier header with the appended one. If they are the same, the TS takes the identifier head as authentic, and goes ahead to prepare the mobile agent for moving. If they are different, the TS knows that the source platform has either maliciously or accidentally modified the identifier header. The TS moves the "bad" mobile agent to place P12 for certain error handling, and records the source platform as a "suspected malicious platform" in its security base through T9. A certain amount of time and space of the TS has to be used to accomplish this process. It is our assumption that all mobile agent platforms are aware of this detection. Therefore, the TS may not need to do the second decryption for every incoming mobile agent. In what situations or relying on what trust models (stored in place P6) the TS should do the second decryption belongs to our future works. Differ-remove arc is used between trust model holder P6 and T5 to make different firing of T5 possible. Figure 21 summarizes the TP process for an incoming mobile agent.

As the detailed path history is recorded by the trust server, if any mobile agent or mobile agent platform tries to deny a migration action which it is involved in, the trust server can prove that this action happened. Therefore non-repudiation can be achieved.

6.1.3   *Mobile agent*

6.1.3.1 *Functionalities and components of a mobile agent*

In our view, a mobile agent is an intelligent software agent that has not only the ability to migrate from one platform to another, but also preserve other behaviors, structures, states, information and goals. It can receive/send messages and data from/to a mobile agent platform as well. A mobile agent's behaviors can be categorized to three actions: reactive action, autonomous action and move action. A reactive action is triggered by a message from outside or a former action of the mobile agent. An autonomous action is initiated by the mobile agent itself when certain conditions hold or it has some goal. Both of them can bring a series of consequent actions. A move action can be either initiated by the mobile agent itself at its will (we call it "active migration"), or invoked by the platform on which this mobile agent resides (we call it "passive migration"). All these actions should be performed with the aid of some security mechanism, and also based on the mobile agent's knowledge base and goal base. Synchronization of these actions is required to guarantee the consistency of certain resource and agent state. Recall the internal/external places and internal/connection transitions we proposed in section 5.3.2.4. A mobile agent is viewed as an object net in EEOS model with in/out communication channels which consist of external places and connects to the outside world through connection transitions. Its knowledge base, goal base, and other places are encapsulated as internal places. Its behavior transitions are treated as internal transitions.

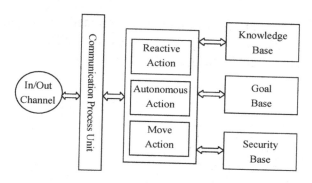

Figure 22 Functionality Components in a Mobile Agent

Based on the above discussion, a generic mobile agent consists of six parts: In/Out communication channel, communication process unit, three actions, knowledge base which stores all information and data this mobile agent knows, goal base which stores the mobile agent's goals and tasks, and security base which provides security mechanism for secure mobile agent migration and execution. Figure 22 illustrates these six parts and the relationship among them. Next we will discuss a mobile agent's communication, migration, and security respectively. The structure of a mobile agent should embed all these three aspects.

6.1.3.2 *EEOS model*

Due to space limitation, a simplified EEOS model of a generic mobile agent is shown in Figure 23. Table 6 is a legend for Figure 23 which shows the meaning and functionality of each place and transition.

It should be noted that most of the transitions in Figure 23 are still high-level abstracted transitions. Some of them are not presented in detail because of the space limitation, such as T3, T8, and T9. While some others, such as T5 and T7 representing "reactive action" and "autonomous action," are in their abstract form because different mobile agents have different actions. It is neither possible nor appropriate to present the detailed structures of those actions in our generic model. We should also mention that the security base represented by place P12 in Figure 23 is connected to each category of action in its abstract form, because a security mechanism should be presented for execution of each action while different security mechanisms work differently and cannot be illustrated in detail in the generic model.

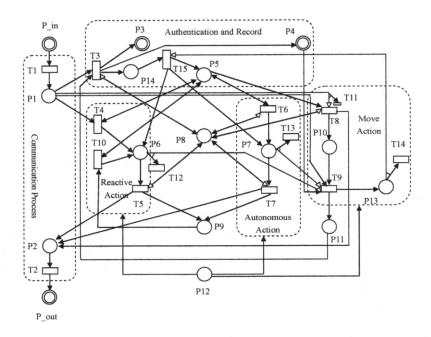

Figure 23 Simplified EEOS Model of a Mobile Agent

Places	Meaning		Transitions	Functions
P1, P2	In/Out communication channel		T1,T2	Process in/out communications
P3	Path history record		T3	Authenticate a MAP, record path history
P4	Current location		T4	Outside message triggers a reactive action
P5	Synchronization		T5	Reactive action
P6	Reactive action tokens holder		T6	Autonomous action initialize
P7	Autonomous action tokens holder		T7	Autonomous action

P8	Knowledge base		T8	Move action initialize
P9	Further action tokens holder		T9	Move action
P10	Move Action tokens holder		T10	Self action triggers a reactive action
P11	Moving state indicator		T11	Move action initialization complement
P12	Security Base		T12	Differ-remove arc transition
P13	State tokens holder		T13	Differ-remove arc transition
P14	Enable token holder		T14	Differ-remove arc transition
			T15	Restore a MA state and enable its execution

Table 6 Legend for Figure 23

In the model, a mobile agent is capable of doing three categories of actions: Reactive actions, autonomous actions and move actions. The invocation of the first two categories of actions can have subsequent reactive actions. This is shown by transition T5 or T7 producing some token to place P9 and resulting in T10 being fired. At any time, only one of the three categories of actions can be initialized. This is indicated in the diagram by the place P5 (Synchronization) whose bound is 1 (the maximum number of tokens in this place is 1). When a mobile agent is initially created, a synchronous token is put in P5. When a reactive action is invoked (either a message-triggered reactive action represented by T4 or a internal-action-triggered reactive action represented by T10), or an autonomous action is initiated (represented by T6), the token is removed from P5. After an action decision has been made, the synchronous token can be restored back to P5. In this way, two goals can be achieved. One is the exclusiveness of making a decision of which action should be performed at any time. The other is the parallelism of performing some actions simultaneously. With respect to move action, since there are two kinds of move actions, we discuss them respectively in the following. Concerning an active migration, the initiation of such an action (represented by T8) takes the token out of place P5. Then the mobile agent proposes its moving request and waits for the permission of its platform. When the permission arrives, it suspends its actions and state (will be discussed in section 6.3.1), and enters its journey. At the same time, the corresponding token in Place P4 (Location) is removed, which indicates that the mobile agent is not currently residing on any platform. Regarding a passive action, we assume that a mobile agent does not refuse the request from its platform to let it move. Invocation of such a passive action (represented by T8||T11) takes the token in place P5 off and sends its agreement to the platform; it waits for the confirmation of the platform. Upon the confirmation arrival, it leaves the platform. Removal of the token in Place P5 in the case of a passive action is similar to that for an active migration discussed above. A token will be put into place P5 again only when a mobile agent arrives at its destination platform and goes through the mutual authentication process (will be introduced in section 6.4.2). For any of the following two cases, say 1) before the mutual authentication process of this mobile agent and any destination platform is finished, e.g. during the travel process of a mobile agent; and 2) if the mutual authentication fails, e.g. a mobile agent travels to an unknown malicious platform and cannot go through the authentication mutually; no synchronous token would be put into place P5 and therefore the actions of the mobile agent are disabled. That helps protect the mobile agent and preserve its state and data.

Let's focus on transition T3 now. It is in its abstract form in the above model. It is refined to several sub transitions to verify the platform's identity when this mobile agent arrives at a mobile agent platform. Afterwards, this transition appends certain information regarding this visit in the form of $< Visit\_Number, time, platform\_identity >$ to place P3 which records the mobile agent's traveling path history. T3 also stores the current mobile agent platform's identity to place P4 to indicate its current location. Then it puts a token in place P14 indicating the mobile agent's execution on this verified platform could be enabled. Transition T15 then picks up the mobile agent's state before it migrates and enables its execution to achieve strong mobility. Since we focus on discussing the mobile agent's structure in this section, how to achieve the strong mobility will be discussed in section 6.3.

P12 is the Security Base for a mobile agent. It is mainly responsible for the secure execution of a mobile agent as the security mechanisms for secure mobile agent migration have been integrated into the structure directly. It holds tokens representing different security mechanisms as object nets. We will come back to this in section 8.5. For security purposes, a mobile agent will drop its path history to the token pool when it leaves a platform for another platform. This is done by transition T16. The details will be introduced in section 6.1.2 and section 6.4.

Pin and Pout are two external full-access places in this model. They are used for communicating with the world outside of this mobile agent. Due to the mobility feature of a mobile agent, its communication with mobile agent platforms is changing over time. Modeling this dynamic communication and connection becomes a challenge which will be addressed in section 6.2. To help with the modeling of dynamic communications and connections, place P4, representing the current location of a mobile agent, is defined as an external read-only place so that its token can be read by other parties, but cannot be changed. Place P2, which holds tokens representing the path history of this mobile agent, is also defined as an external place so that the mobile agent can drop a copy of its current path history to a trusted server for security purpose (details in section 6.4).

From Figure 23 and Table 6 , we can identify a list of behaviors of a mobile agent supported by our EEOS model.

1. Autonomous action: $P8 + P5 \rightarrow T6 \rightarrow P7(+ P8) \rightarrow T7$
2. Reactive action:
    (2.1) Invoked by message from outside:
    $P1 + P5 \rightarrow T4 \rightarrow P6 (+ P8) \rightarrow T5$
    (2.2) Triggered by other inner action:
    $P9 + P5 \rightarrow T10 \rightarrow P6 (+ P8) \rightarrow T5$
3. Move action:
    (3.1) Depart:
        (3.1.1) Active migration:

$$P8 + P5 \rightarrow T8 \rightarrow P10(P1 + P4 + P13)[+P6 + P7] \rightarrow$$
$$T9[+T12 + T13] \rightarrow P11 + P13$$

(3.1.2) Passive migration:

$$P8 + P5[+P1] \rightarrow T8[+T11] \rightarrow P10(P1 + P4 + P13)$$
$$[+P6 + P7] \rightarrow T9[+T12 + T13] \rightarrow P11 + P13$$

(3.2) Arrive:
$$P1 + P11 + P8[+P13] \rightarrow T3 \rightarrow P3 + P4 + P5 \mid P6 \mid P7$$
4. Communication:
    (4.1) Out-going: $T5 \mid T7 \mid T8 \rightarrow P2 \rightarrow T2 \rightarrow Pout$
    (4.2) In-coming: $Pin \rightarrow T1 \rightarrow P1 \rightarrow T3 \mid T4 \mid T9 \mid T8 \mid T11$
5. Subsequent action: $T5 \mid T7 \rightarrow P9 \rightarrow T10$

6.2 Communication in a Mobile Agent System

Communications in a generic secure mobile agent system are pretty complicated because of the following reasons: 1) Communications between mobile agents and mobile agent platforms are based on their connection relation, which is dynamically changed; 2) Communication styles are different for mobile agents and mobile agent platforms, for example, mobile agent platforms have external and internal communications while mobile agents only have external communications; 3) Communications can be synchronous and asynchronous for different situations; 4) Communication contents are quite different for different sessions and different entities; and 5) Communications should be secure. Therefore, we propose a set of mechanisms to support the modeling of the communications as well as building secure communications.

6.2.1 *Dynamic connection*

A mobile agent can only communicate with the mobile agent platform it is currently residing on. When a mobile agent is on a mobile agent platform, the communications between this mobile agent and other parties should be through this platform both practically and for security purposes. If a mobile agent MA transfers to a mobile agent platform

MAP, a communication channel between MA and MAP should be established. Once MA leaves MAP, this communication should be disconnected. But since the structure of an EEOS cannot be changed dynamically, we have to figure out another way to model this kind of dynamic connection.

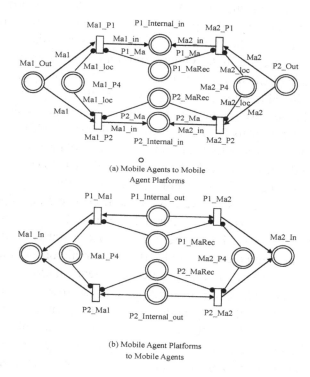

(a) Mobile Agents to Mobile
Agent Platforms

(b) Mobile Agent Platforms
to Mobile Agents

Figure 24 Dynamic Connections and Communications

In our EEOS model, we use the following method to achieve this goal. Structurally, a mobile agent's "In" communication channel is connected to each mobile agent platform's "Internal_out" communication channel, and a mobile agent's "Out" communication channel is connected to each mobile agent platform's "Internal_in" communication channel through *"exclusively conditioned transitions"*. Internal communication channels of a mobile agent platform are used because a mobile agent can only start to communicate with a mobile agent platform after it arrives at the platform and therefore their communications belong to internal communications for that platform. "Exclusively conditioned transitions", as the name suggests, are transitions whose enabling conditions are exclusive. If one transition gets enabled and fired, other transitions which have the exclusively conditioned relationship with this transition are definitely disabled. Behaviorally, for a mobile agent, at any time only the communication channels to one of the mobile agent platforms on which the mobile agent resides are through. Other communication channels to other platforms are blocked because the exclusive conditions guarantee that transitions linked to other platforms cannot be fired.

To make our discussion concrete, we use a system consisting of two mobile agent platforms P1, P2 and two mobile agents Ma1, Ma2. Figure 24 illustrates the structure of the complete connection. Transitions Ma1_P1 and Ma1_P2, Ma2_P1 and Ma2_P2, P1_Ma1 and P2_Ma1, P1_Ma2 and P2_Ma2 are four pairs of exclusively conditioned transitions. There are also exclusive conditioned relationships between Ma1_P1 and P2_Ma1, Ma1_P2 and P1_Ma1, Ma2_P1 and P2_Ma2, Ma2_P2 and P1_Ma2. Firing these transitions or not controls the flow of the actual communications and reflects the real connections between the mobile agents and certain mobile agent platforms. Exclusive conditions include judging a mobile agent's current location, and the source and destination of a message. A mobile agent's current location is determined by both the "location record" place of a mobile agent and the "mobile agents recording" place of a mobile agent platform. Only when the contents in these two places match with each other can the belief that this mobile agent resides on that mobile agent platform be established. For example, mobile agent Ma1 is currently on platform P2 and Ma1 sends a request to P2. This request should include P2's identifier in its content body and the mobile agents recording place of platform P2 (P2_MaRec) also contains a token indicating Ma1. In the case, only transition Ma1_P2 is enabled and firing it results in the request leaving Ma1_Out for P2_In. For example, both Ma1 and Ma2 are on platform P1 and Ma1 wants to send a message to P1. In this case, Ma1_P4 holds P1's identifier and P1_MaRec holds Ma1's identifier so that they can match. In addition, Ma2_P4 holds P1's identifier and

P1_MaRec also holds Ma2's identifier so that they can match as well. But the message is from Ma1 to P1, so only transition Ma1_P1 is enabled and can be fired. Its exclusively conditioned transitions Ma1_P2 and P2_Ma1 are disabled because of the exclusiveness, which guarantees that Ma1 will not have a chance to directly communicate with P2.

6.2.2 *Communications for a mobile agent platform and a mobile agent*

6.2.2.1 *Communication contents*

Communications on a mobile agent platform are differentiated to two categories: external communication and internal communication. The former refers to the communications between a mobile agent platform and its outside world including other platforms, the token pool and third parties. The latter refers to the communications between this mobile agent platform and agents on it (including stationary agents and mobile agents). Both external and internal communications can support synchronous and asynchronous communications.

Generally speaking, external communications include two kinds of information, encrypted mobile agents and encrypted data/messages. A mobile agent platform can receive a mobile agent in its encrypted form from the token pool. When this mobile agent finishes its tasks, it leaves the mobile agent platform to the token pool in its encrypted form again, and this encryption form is different from the one when the mobile agent arrives. We will discuss the secure transportation of mobile agents in more details in section 6.4.1. In this section, we will focus on the communications of data and messages. A mobile agent platform MAP_A can communicate with another mobile agent platform MAP_B, and agents residing on MAP_B through MAP_B. An agent on MAP_A can communicate with another agent on MAP_B through these two platforms. One principle of communications is that an agent on a mobile agent platform can only communicate with this platform directly, while all other communications between this agent and other agents or platforms must be through this platform. Therefore, when platform MAP_A intends to communicate with a mobile agent MA on MAP_B, it can only send messages to MAP_B instead of MA directly. MAP_B then forwards the messages to MA through its internal communication channel. It is the same for the communication in the other direction from MA to MAP_A that MAP_B also acts as the communication intermediary. In this way, MAP_A will not be able to interfere with the relationship between MA and MAP_B. By filtering the messages from outside, MAP_B can eliminate some insecure communications. For example, when MAP_A fakes as MAP_B or sends a message to MA asking it to do some harm to MAP_B, MAP_B can detect that and avoid being faked or attacked by not forwarding the malicious message to MA. The other side, if MAP_B modifies a message between MAP_A and MA maliciously, belongs to our future consideration. A piece of general information running in the external communication channel has the following format: $(source\_plat, destination\_plat, style, body)_{pub\_key}$. As the names indicate, $source\_plat$ refers to the source platform this piece of information comes from; $destination\_plat$ refers to the destination platform this information goes to; $style$ varies the content of this information and $body$ is the concrete content of this information. pub_key is the public key of the destination platform used to encrypt this information to achieve security. After a mobile agent platform receives a piece of information and decrypts it successfully, it identifies the style first and acts differently according to the style.

Style	Body
1	Encrypted mobile agent, in the form of (<HPI, SI, MA>)
2	Encrypted Message/data/synchronization between platforms, in the form of (info)
3	Encrypted Message/data between platform and agent on other platform, in the form of (agent_id, info)
4	Encrypted Message/data between local agents and agents on other platform, in the form of (source_agent_id, destination_agent_id, info)

Table 7 Styles and Bodies for External Communications

Table 7 shows different styles and message bodies. For example, if MA_A on MAP_A wants to send a message "ready" to MA_B on MAP_B, the message $(MAP_A, MAP_B, 4, MA_A, MA_B, "ready")_{pub\_key}$ is constructed and sent from MAP_A to MAP_B with the aid of token pool.

Style	Body
1	Encrypted mobile agent platform ID from *plat* to *agent*, in the form of (<Plat_identifier>$_{pkey}$)
2	Message/data/synchronization from *plat* to *agent*, in the form of (info)
3	Message/data/synchronization from *agent* to *plat*, in the form of (info)

Table 8 Internal Communication Styles and Bodies

As discussed in section 6.2.1, the internal communication channel of a mobile agent platform is dynamically connected to the communication channels of mobile agents. The dynamicity is achieved by constructing a complete connection structure and firing exclusively conditioned transition based on the location of a mobile agent and the destination of the communication information. After a mobile agent platform receives a mobile agent successfully, it records the mobile agent in place P7 (same functionality as place P1_MaRec in Figure 24). Correspondingly, this mobile agent also records the mobile agent platform as its current location. Afterwards, the dynamic communications between the mobile agent and the mobile agent platform is established. A general message in the internal communication channel has the following format: $(agent, plat, style, body)$ which content is shown in Table 8.

For example, MAP_A wants to send a message "ask to move" to a mobile agent MA1 on it. It constructs a message $(MA1, MAP_A, 2, "ask\_to\_move")$ and sends the message to place P_{io}. Because MA1 is recorded in MAP_A's P7, MAP_A is also recorded in MA1's P4, and this message in P_{io} is to MA, it will be forwarded to the incoming communication channel of the mobile agent MA object net.

6.2.2.2 Synchronous and asynchronous communications

We have mentioned before that the communications in a mobile agent system can be both synchronous and asynchronous. This is true for both external and internal communications in certain situations. In this section, we use internal communications to discuss the synchronous and asynchronous communications. A communication session to reach an agreement for a mobile agent migration, which can be an active migration or passive migration, involves synchronous communications between a mobile agent and a mobile agent platform. Communication sessions to send certain data between a mobile agent and its platform usually involve asynchronous communications. Asynchronous communication is the default communication to enable maximum parallelism. When synchronous communication is desired, the sender of a message should send synchronization to the receiver. After the receiver also replies synchronization to the sender, the synchronous communication can be set up. Afterwards, the sender sends a message or data to the receiver and blocks its execution until it receives the acknowledgement from the receiver. The receiver blocks its execution until it receives the message or data from the sender, and sends an acknowledgement right away. After the synchronous communication is over, communication style returns to asynchronous communication, where sender doesn't block for acknowledgement and receiver doesn't automatically send the acknowledgment after it receives something.

In synchronous communication, a sender will remove the message just sent from the sending buffer once it receives the acknowledgement from the receiver for this message. And a receiver moves the message it receives from the receiving buffer once it receives it. Therefore the sending buffer and receiving buffer is not in danger of overflowing. Figure 25 illustrates the synchronous communication.

Asynchronous communication is different such that a receiving buffer may be overflow because a sender may send too much information to the receiving buffer before the receiver picks them up. Therefore we should add a testing mechanism to asynchronous communication. As Figure 26 illustrates, a transition is connected to the receiving buffer through testing arc and tests whether the receiving buffer is full. If it is, it will record this condition to the "Receiving buffer full" place, which is connected to the "send message" transition through an inhibitor arc. Therefore if the receiving buffer is full, the "send message" transition will be disabled so that no more messages will be sent to that buffer to avoid having the buffer overflow.

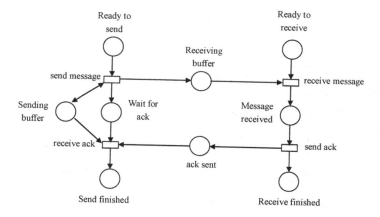

Figure 25 Synchronous Communications

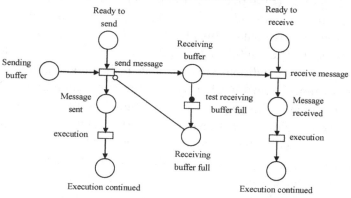

Figure 26 Asynchronous Communication

The communication sessions between a mobile agent and a mobile agent platform on which this mobile agent resides to reach an agreement for a mobile agent migration involve several synchronous communications for each message exchanged. The sessions are shown in Figure 27 which is an agent UML sequence diagram. Figure 27 (a) is for active migration in which the mobile agent requests to move; (b) is for passive migration in which the mobile agent platform asks the mobile agent to move.

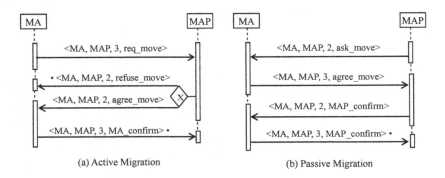

(a) Active Migration   (b) Passive Migration

Figure 27 Communications for mobile agent migration agreement

In Figure 27 (a) active migration, a mobile agent sends a request message to its current mobile agent platform and expresses its willingness to move out of this platform (refer to Table 8 for the format of messages). The mobile agent platform can choose to reject this request if certain conditions are met, such as the outgoing mobile agents holder are almost overflowed or the network connection failed. Or it can choose to agree to this request. The "x" signal in the decision diamond indicates an exclusive-or decision [181]. If the mobile agent platform refuses this request, the communication ends, which is indicated by a terminator signal "•". Otherwise, after the mobile agent receives the agreement from the platform, it sends a confirmation message to the platform and ends this communication. In Figure 27 (b) passive migration, a mobile agent platform asks a mobile agent on it to leave. In our current model, a mobile agent always agrees because it does not have the control for staying. Then the mobile agent platform sends a confirmation to this mobile agent and waits for the confirmation from the mobile agent as the termination of this communication. In either case, a mobile agent platform needs the confirmation from a mobile agent as a proof for non-repudiation.

6.3   Mobility in a Mobile Agent System

The most distinct characteristic of a mobile agent is its mobility. A mobile agent can decide when and where it should go to accomplish its tasks. In this case, the mobile agent mobility is active. A mobile agent can also be asked to go somewhere at sometime by the mobile agent platform it currently resides on. In this case, the mobile agent mobility is passive. No matter whether a mobile agent migrates to another platform actively or passively, its transfer causes transfer of different information in the network. A mobile agent, which is a software program, consists of code, data and state. If only code and data of a mobile agent get transferred when this mobile agent migrates, then we call this kind of mobility as "weak mobility". If all three parts transfer when the mobile agent migrates, then we call it as "strong mobility". Strong mobility and strong migration are both required for different application areas. Therefore our modeling supports both forms of migration. We start with strong mobility. By eliminating the parts to capture and restore mobile agent state, weak mobility can be achieved.

6.3.1   *Strong mobility*

In our opinion, a mobile agent transfer includes the following three stages: a mobile agent requests to move out of the current platform or a platform asks a mobile agent to leave; a mobile agent is transferred from one platform to another; and a mobile agent arrives at another platform. We call these three stages as pre-transfer stage, transfer stage, and post-transfer stage respectively.

1. Pre-transfer stage

When a mobile agent is executed on a mobile agent platform and needs to go to some other platform to fulfill its execution, it submits a request to its current platform to move. Or if a mobile agent platform wants a mobile agent on it to go somewhere, it will send a message to this mobile agent asking it to leave. The internal communications between a mobile agent and a mobile agent platform were introduced in section 6.2.2.2. We use the active migration to discuss the pre-transfer stage in this section and it is similar for the passive migration case. A mobile agent can include its destination into its request to move, or send it in another message. The destination could be just a single machine (in single-hop case) or a group of computers (in multi-hop case). After the mobile agent platform receives this request, approves it and receives the confirmation from the mobile agent again, an agreement for the mobile agent migration is achieved.

We introduced the procedure of a mobile agent platform to prepare an outgoing mobile agent in section 6.1.1.2.2. This method enforces the security level of the mobile agent system in the following aspects. First of all, the body of a mobile agent would not be modified meaningfully during its travel since it is encrypted. Even if some malicious party changes it randomly, it cannot be restored to it original executable state by performing the normal decryption. Secondly, a mobile agent is encrypted by its home platform's private key. When the destination platform receives this mobile agent, it can confirm which platform this mobile agent comes from. Thirdly, by restricting the distribution of public keys within a trusted network, we can avoid the attack from platforms which are outside this network to some extent. The shortcomings of this method may include possible cost increase such as time for encryption and decryption.

A mobile agent platform communicates with other platforms and the trust server through its external communication channels. As introduced in section 6.2.2.2, the external communications can be synchronous and asynchronous. In the case of transporting a mobile agent, a mobile agent platform always communicates with the trust server directly using synchronous communications.

Once a mobile agent is put into a waiting queue to transfer, its functionality should be disabled. This condition prevents the inconsistency that might occur when the state and data of a mobile agent are allowed to vary during the transferring process. A mobile agent's current state should be captured so that when it arrives at another platform, its state can be restored and its execution can start from the exact point before it leaves the previous platform. These two points are associated with each other. The execution state of a mobile agent includes its stack and program counter. In our EEOS model for a mobile agent as shown in Figure 23, all the variables in the stack are stored in place P8 (Knowledge Base). Therefore when the mobile agent transfers, as long as the marking of P8 doesn't change, the variables would not be changed either. From Figure 23, we can see that transitions which are connected to place P8 (therefore can change marking of P8) are T3, T5, T6, T7, T8. T3 is fired only when a mobile agent arrives at a mobile agent platform and receives the encrypted form of the platform's identifier. It uses the public key of the destination platform stored in its Knowledge Base (Place P8) for decryption and getting the identifier of the mobile agent platform (details in section 6.4). Therefore, firing T3 should not change the values of the stack variables. But if there are certain tokens in place P6 and P7, transition T5 and T7 may be enabled. Consequently they can change the marking of P8 and enable further action by putting a synchronous token back into place P5. It is obviously not desired. On the other hand, the program counter value, which tells a processor which statement of a program is going to be executed, should also be taken into consideration. Reflected in our EEOS model of a mobile agent, the program counter value tells which action transition is going to be fired. This execution flow is controlled by the markings of places P6, P7, P8. As we discussed above, the markings of these three places may be changed since certain transition (T6 or T7) may be enabled and fired during a mobile agent's transfer.

To solve the two problems mentioned above and support strong mobility modeling, we introduce the *remove-restore mechanism* to our EEOS modeling of a mobile agent. This mechanism is realized by the subparts in Figure 23 shown in section 6.3.1. This mechanism removes all tokens in place P6 and P7 (if there is any) to disable the execution of its reactive and autonomous actions thus to preserve its execution state, and records the markings of these two places in another place P13 when a mobile agent requests to move or is asked to move. If there is no token in these two places, transition T8 can still be fired since we can use the "differ-remove" arcs between transition T8 and place P6/P7. After a mobile agent arrives at its destination platform, decrypts the platform's identifier and the mutual authentication process is accomplished, transition T3 restores tokens to place P6 and P7 according to the state record in place P13, and puts a synchronous token to place P5 to enable this mobile agent's execution as well. If there is no token in P13 which indicates there is no token in place P6 and P7, transition T3 simply does the latter part. In this way, we can make sure that a mobile agent starts execution on a new mobile agent platform exactly from the point when it leaves the previous mobile agent platform. Therefore, strong mobility is achieved.

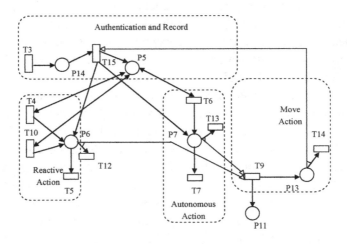

Figure 28 "Remove-restore" mechanism for strong mobility in Figure 23

2. Transfer stage

When a mobile agent platform is ready to send mobile agents, it sends out the mobile agent which is in the head of its outgoing mobile agent queue to the network, in the similar way it sends out normal data or message. The first destination of the mobile agent should always be the trust server, which will perform a sequence of security checks and process. And then the trusted server will encrypt the packed mobile agent using the public key of the destination platform. The details of the trusted server were introduced in section 6.1.2. Afterwards, the mobile agent leaves for its destination platform. It is disabled in a token pool.

That guarantees that the mobile agent should not change its state and data (as well as its code) before normal arrival and being executed again.

3. Post-transfer stage

When a mobile agent platform receives the packed mobile agent in its encrypted form from network, it performs a sequence of actions. Firstly, it decrypted the mobile agent with its private key. In our framework, a mobile agent platform always receives a mobile agent from the trust server which checks the security of the mobile agent and encrypts it using the public key of the destination platform. Therefore, only the intended destination platform can correctly decrypts the mobile agent under the assumption that no one else knows its private key. After this decryption, the destination platform identity, the current path history, and the unique identifier pair of the mobile agent become clear-text. Secondly, the mobile agent platform checks the identifier pair with the aid of its security base in which a "dangerous-party list" is maintained. Only when the check is passed with no problem, will the platform decrypt the rest of the information using the public key of the host platform of this mobile agent and then goes through the registration process for the mobile agent. Thirdly, according to the result of the registration, the mobile agent platform either accepts and authorizes a mobile agent if it can be trusted, or freezes the mobile agent if it is suspected. For the former, the mobile agent platform puts the mobile agent to be executed into its "ready" queue and sends its own platform identifier encrypted using its private key to the mobile agent for mutual authentication. For the latter, the mobile agent platform can choose to kill the malicious mobile agent if necessary.

After the three steps mentioned above, a trusted incoming mobile agent token is placed into place P6. As a mobile agent's execution state is firstly restored by the platform based on the state tokens it carries, the strong mobility can be achieved. Now it is ready to be executed by transition T8 as refined in Figure 19. The mobile agent platform may create its own mobile agent and put it into place P6 for execution by T8 as well. Such mobile agent may be executed in a similar way to that of a foreign mobile agent. In a normal case, a mobile agent created by a certain mobile agent platform should not be malicious towards this mobile agent platform before moving to anywhere.

6.3.2 *Weak mobility*

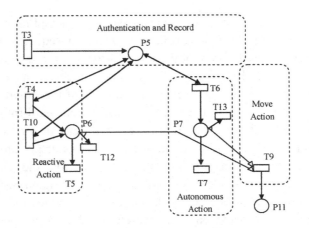

Figure 29 "Remove" mechanism for weak mobility

The most distinct difference between strong mobility and weak mobility of a mobile agent is whether the execution state of a mobile agent will be captured when this mobile agent is leaving a mobile agent platform and whether the state can be restored when this mobile agent starts execution on another mobile agent platform. Therefore, based on our EEOS models for mobile agents and mobile agent platforms, to achieve weak mobility, we will eliminate the parts for "remove-restore" mechanism.

However, it is not enough to model weak mobility if we just simply take off the "remove-restore" mechanism. If there are certain tokens in place P6 or P7 in Figure 23 and they remain there when the mobile agent migrates, transition T5 or T7 may be fired which is contradictory to our assumption that a mobile agent's functions should be disabled when it is traveling. Therefore we should remove those tokens before the mobile agent leaves the original platform. But we do not save them because for weak mobility the execution state does not travel with the mobile agent. Therefore when this mobile agent arrives at a new mobile agent platform, its previous execution state is not preserved. It will get a synchronous token in place P5 if it goes through the mutual authentication and identifiers check successfully. When it gets the processor to execute, its execution state is based on the code and data it carries, not its previous state. This is exactly what "weak mobility" means. We call the mechanism to remove tokens in place P6 and P7 as "remove" mechanism and illustrate it in Figure 29. When the "remove-restore" mechanism is replaced by the "remove" mechanism in Figure 23, the corresponding mobile agent can only be capable of strong mobility. For the mobile agent platform model, only the place "RestoreState" in Figure 19 for mobile agent execution needs to be eliminated to support weak mobility.

6.3.3 *Discussion about weak mobility and strong mobility*

Strong mobility is at the heart of mobile agent technology because when a mobile agent leaves a mobile agent platform, it should suspend its state and resume the state after it arrives at another mobile agent platform. Weak mobility actually does not abide by this principle. But weak mobility is also desired due to the following reasons.

One reason is that it is easier to implement weak mobility in applications. Java is probably the most popular programming language to implement mobile agent system because Java only provides weak mobility. In Java, an agent is implemented by a thread and one or more objects. Since it is very hard to extract the inner structures of a thread, the execution state of a thread cannot be saved and restored. Many mobile agent systems are built in Java, such as Mole, Odyssey, and Aglets. Therefore they can only support "strong" mobility without consideration of the execution state of a thread. Although some other systems support strong mobility (like Telescrip, Agent Tcl), they have to use dedicated language interpreter to capture and resume the process execution state. To implement such systems, additional code should be programmed to store the stack values and program counter of a mobile agent, then to transfer those values together with the mobile agent. On the other hand, a mobile agent platform should also pay special attention to resume those state values transferred with a mobile agent. So from the aspect of cost, weak mobility is cheaper.

The second reason is that a mobile agent with strong mobility is more prone to be attacked. By spying on the execution state of a mobile agent, a malicious party can eavesdrop confidential information of this mobile agent and even the mobile agent platforms the mobile agent visited. By modifying the execution state of a mobile agent, a malicious party can easily change the behavior of this mobile agent. From the aspect of security, weak mobility is at a lower risk.

Another reason is that strong mobility is not necessary for many applications. Information retrieval, electronic commerce, network management, and load balancing are applications which use mobile agent technology most. In information retrieval, the same retrieval procedure is performed after a mobile agent moves to each platform, and the results from the procedure are stored as data and transferred with the mobile agent. Therefore how the procedure is performed and the execution state of this mobile agent on a certain mobile agent platform are of no interest for the whole system. In electronic commerce, a mobile agent goes to some other platforms to find some information on behalf of its home platform. The home platform usually makes a decision after the mobile agent it dispatches comes back with collected data. Hence the execution state of the mobile agent is not required to transfer with the mobile agent. It is similar in the network management field that weak mobility is also enough since the management of a network node depends on the local environment of that node only. But the situation is different in the field of load balancing, since the execution state of a mobile agent, searching for computational resource in a network and migrating to a mobile agent platform with such resource, should be exactly the same as its execution state before the migration. Otherwise the computation of this mobile agent makes no sense. Therefore we can see for many applications, weak mobility is enough.

From the above discussion, we can conclude that although strong mobility is more complete and essential to mobile agent technology, weak mobility is also desired in certain situation. That is why we provide support for both of them in our models.

6.4 Security in a Mobile Agent System

As introduced in section 4.1, many security problems exist in a mobile agent system. Our thesis does not aim to solve all of them. Our focus is on secure mobile agent migration, mutual authentication between a mobile agent and a mobile agent platform, authorization for a mobile agent to use system resources, and mobile agent data security as well as action security. Before we introduce them in detail, it is necessary to briefly introduce the public-key cryptography because it is the basis for most of the security mechanisms in our framework.

To formalize the transfer and authenticate processes which we will introduce in the following sections, we use the following formalizations shown in Table 9. From those formalisms, we may infer some expression. For example, we have $f_{dec}(f_{enc}(x,y),y') = x \Leftrightarrow asy(y,y') \equiv 1 \vee asy(y',y) \equiv 1$ where $\Leftrightarrow$ means "if and only iff".

Formalism	Meaning
MA_i	Mobile agent i
MA_Id_i	The identifier of mobile agent i
MAP_j	Mobile agent platform j
MAP_Id_j	The identifier of mobile agent platform j
$pubkey_x$	The public key of entity x
$prikey_x$	The private key of entity x
$asy(x,y) \equiv 1$	x and y are two asymmetric keys for certain entity t such that $x = pubkey_t$ and $y = pubkey_t$
$f_{app}(x,y) = <x,y>$	Append x in front of y, and the result is written as $<x,y>$
$f_{enc}(x,y) = \{x\}_y$	Encrypt x using y as the encryption key, and the result is written as $\{x\}_y$
$f_{dec}(x,y)$	Decrypt x using y as the decryption key
$f_{pair}(x,y) = x \| y$	Combine x, y as a pair, and the result is written as $x \| y$
$f_{ex\_h}(<x,y>) = x$	Extract the head of some appended information
$f_{ex\_t}(<x,y>) = y$	Extract the tail of some appended information

$f_{cp}(x,y) \Rightarrow y = x$	Copy x to y such that $y = x$

Table 9 Formalisms for Public-key Cryptography-based Security Mechanisms

6.4.1   *Secure mobile agent transfer*

With the help of the TS, secure mobile agent transfers can be achieved. The "secure mobile agent transfer" here does not mean we can guarantee that any mobile agent can arrive at its destination securely. Actually our model (and probably almost all practical mobile agent systems) cannot prevent a mobile agent from being lost or modified during its journey. What we can guarantee is two-folded. One is that we can make sure the mobile agent arriving at the destination platform (or TS) and passing the decryption is really the original mobile agent. The other is that if a mobile agent has been modified during its way before it arrives at the destination platform (or TS), it can be detected so that it will not be executed or forwarded to other places.

Firstly, the mobile agent platform, which will dispatch a mobile agent, encrypts and packs the mobile agents as illustrated in Figure 18, then sends it to the TS. During the mobile agent traveling from the platform to the TS, even if the encrypted mobile agent is intercepted by some other malicious mobile agent platform, it cannot be decrypted because no one except the TS itself has the private key to decrypt the mobile agent correctly. Then a malicious mobile agent platform may choose to change the encrypted mobile agent randomly as an attack. For this situation, after the mobile agent reaches the TS, TS decrypts the mobile agent using its own private key. Since the message body of this mobile agent has been changed, the result after decryption either does not abide by the formulation, or causes inconsistency during the check. For example, the identifier of the platform after decryption exceeds the range of valid platform identifiers. So the TS can detect the change and mark the mobile agent as "dangerous". Obviously, the TS will not forward it to any platform and instead the TS performs some special handling of this error. In addition, the TS can verify the source platform from which the mobile agent came by decrypting the mobile agent at the second level using the public key of the claimed source platform of this mobile agent. Actually the encrypted mobile agent using the private key of the source platform acts as a digital signature of the platform. If this decryption can go through correctly, the source platform is verified.

Secondly, if the mobile agent passes through all the decryptions and checks on the TS, the TS will encrypt it using the public key of the destination platform and dispatch it to that platform. If the mobile agent arrives at that destination platform without being attacked during its journey, the destination platform can use its private key and decrypt the mobile agent correctly. It can then go ahead and authenticate this mobile agent. However, if the mobile agent has been changed on its way to the destination, similar to what we discussed above for the TS, the destination platform can detect the possible violation of the formulation or inconsistency. If such violation of inconsistency happens, the destination platform has reason to suspect the trustworthiness of this mobile agent and may put the mobile agent into its "Prison".

Thirdly, to reinforce the secure transfer, mobile agent platforms and the TS will reach an agreement to transfer a mobile agent by using synchronous communications before the transfer is made. If the TS agrees with a mobile agent platform on receiving a mobile agent but doesn't receive it after a certain amount of time, or a platform receives a mobile agent without granting any agreement with the TS for receiving it before, the TS or the platform knows something bad happened. For the former situation, the mobile agent might be lost or intercepted by a malicious party, or might be delayed by crowded network transportation. The TS may interact with the mobile agent platform sending the mobile agent to investigate further. For the latter, a malicious mobile agent platform may try to bypass the security check of the TS and send a malicious mobile agent to the platform directly. The platform can interact with the TS to verify this mobile agent transfer has not been registered and scheduled on the TS. Therefore the platform can select to ignore this mobile agent, freeze it or even discard it.

In this way, both the source platform and the destination platform of a mobile agent can be verified and the mobile agent remains encrypted on its way from one platform to another except on the trusted server. A mobile agent either arrives at its destination platform without being attacked and gets authenticated and executed afterwards; or arrives at the TS or the destination platform being attacked, detected and denied execution. Therefore the secure mobile agent transfer can be achieved.

In the following, we will talk a little bit more about the public key. The trusted server TS should obtain the public keys of all registered mobile agent platforms, while a mobile agent platform does not need to keep the public keys of all other platforms. When a mobile agent platform needs to decrypt the mobile agent from another platform using the public key of that platform, but it does not have the public key, it will send a request to the trusted server TS asking for that public key. Depending on different situations, the TS can choose to send the public key of the source platform of the mobile agent to the destination platform through symmetric cryptograph if a secure channel between the TS and the destination platform exist, or through asymmetric cryptograph otherwise. The TS will also keep record of which mobile agent platform has asked for which other platforms' public keys. This can help with reducing the space used for restoring public keys of other platforms in a mobile agent platform. It also saves time and trouble when a mobile agent platform decides to change its private-public keys and needs to update its public keys saved on other platforms. For this situation, the mobile agent platform simply sends an update notice and the new public key to the TS and the TS will do the necessary updates for it. In addition, the TS can restrict the distribution of the public keys to only trust-worthy platforms. The TS may maintain a "malicious mobile agent platform list". If a platform is found and proved malicious, the TS will record it into the list. Any request of public keys of other platforms from the platforms in this list will be denied. Mobile agents from those platforms in this list will also be treated specially under more serious security check if they are not denied at all.

If the mobile agent system network is very large and having only one trusted server for transferring mobile agents is not enough, we may set up several trusted servers which cooperate with each other to achieve the goals. How to decide the individual responsibilities of those trusted servers and how those trusted servers can cooperate with each other belong to our future works.

6.4.1.1 *Formalization of the secure mobile agent transfer*

Using the formalisms we introduced in the beginning of this chapter, we can specify the secure mobile agent transfer formally as follows. Suppose a mobile agent i created by mobile agent platform j is transferring from mobile agent platform m to another mobile agent platform n via the trusted server TS.

1. The mobile agent platform m will do the following:

$$f_{enc}(f_{app}(MAP\_Id_n, f_{app}(MAP\_Id_m, f_{app}(f_{pair}(MAP\_Id_j, MA\_Id_i,$$
$$f_{enc}(MA_i, prikey_{MAP\_Id_m})))), pubkey_{TS})$$
$$= \{< MAP\_Id_n, < MAP\_Id_m, < MAP\_Id_j \|$$
$$MAP\_Id_i, \{MA_i\}_{prikey_{MAP\_Id_m}} >>> \}_{pubkey_{TS}}$$

and send it to the trusted server.

2. After the trusted server receives this packed and encrypted mobile agent, it will use $asy(pubkey_{TS}, prikey_{TS}) \equiv 1$ and do:

(1) Decrypting the mobile agent at the first level:

$$f_{dec}(\{< MAP\_Id_n, < MAP\_Id_m, < MAP\_Id_j \|$$
$$MAP\_Id_i, \{MA_i\}_{prikey_{MAP\_Id_m}} >>> \}_{pubkey_{TS}}, prikey_{TS}) =$$
$$< MAP\_Id_n, < MAP\_Id_m, < MAP\_Id_j \|$$
$$MAP\_Id_i, \{MA_i\}_{prikey_{MAP\_Id_m}} >>>$$

(2) Extracting:

$$f_{ex\_h}(< MAP\_Id_n, < MAP\_Id_m, < MAP\_Id_j \|$$
$$MAP\_Id_i, \{MA_i\}_{prikey_{MAP\_Id_m}} >>>) = MAP\_Id_n$$

$$f_{ex\_h}(f_{ex\_t}(< MAP\_Id_n, < MAP\_Id_m, < MAP\_Id_j \parallel$$
$$MAP\_Id_i, \{MA_i\}_{prikey_{MAP\_Id_m}} >>>)) = MAP\_Id_m$$

$$f_{ex\_h}(f_{ex\_t}(f_{ex\_t}(< MAP\_Id_n, < MAP\_Id_m, < MAP\_Id_j \parallel$$
$$MAP\_Id_i, \{MA_i\}_{prikey_{MAP\_Id_m}} >>>))) = MAP\_Id_j \parallel MA\_Id$$

as the destination platform identifier, the source platform identifier and the identifiers pair of the mobile agent for check up and registration.

(3) Using $asy(pubkey_{MAP\_Id_m}, prikey_{MAP\_Id_m}) \equiv 1$ to decrypt the mobile agent on the second level:

$$f_{cp}(f_{ex\_t}(f_{ex\_t}(f_{ex\_t}(< MAP\_Id_n, < MAP\_Id_m, < MAP\_Id_j \parallel$$
$$MAP\_Id_i, \{MA_i\}_{prikey_{MAP\_Id_m}} >>>))), y) \Rightarrow y = \{MA_i\}_{prikey_{MAP\_Id_m}}$$

$$f_{dec}(f_{ex\_t}(f_{ex\_t}(f_{ex\_t}(< MAP\_Id_n, < MAP\_Id_m, < MAP\_Id_j \parallel$$
$$MAP\_Id_i, \{MA_i\}_{prikey_{MAP\_Id_m}} >>>))), pubkey_{MAP\_Id_m}) = MA_i$$

to get the clear-text form of the mobile agent for further check up.

(4) Encrypting the mobile agent as follows:

$$f_{enc}(f_{app}(MAP\_Id_n, f_{app}(MAP\_Id_m, f_{app}(f_{pair}(MAP\_Id_j,$$
$$MA\_Id_i), y))), pubkey_{MAP\_Id_n})$$
$$= \{< MAP\_Id_n, < MAP\_Id_m, < MAP\_Id_j \parallel$$
$$MAP\_Id_i, \{MA_i\}_{prikey_{MAP\_Id_m}} >>>\}_{pubkey_{MAP\_Id_n}}$$

and send the packed and encrypted mobile agent to the destination mobile agent platform n.

3. After receiving this mobile agent, the platform n will do:

(1) Decrypting the mobile agent by using:

$$asy(pubkey_{MAP\_Id_n}, prikey_{MAP\_Id_n}) \equiv 1$$

and doing:

$$f_{dec}(\{< MAP\_Id_n, < MAP\_Id_m, < MAP\_Id_j \|$$
$$MAP\_Id_i, \{MA_i\}_{prikey_{MAP\_Id_m}} >>>\}_{pubkey_{MAP\_Id_n}}, prikey_{MAP\_Id_n}) =$$
$$< MAP\_Id_n, < MAP\_Id_m, < MAP\_Id_j \|$$
$$MAP\_Id_i, \{MA_i\}_{prikey_{MAP\_Id_m}} >>>$$

(2) Extracting the destination platform, the source platform and the identifiers pair of the mobile agent for check up by doing:

$$f_{ex\_h}(< MAP\_Id_n, < MAP\_Id_m, < MAP\_Id_j \|$$
$$MAP\_Id_i, \{MA_i\}_{prikey_{MAP\ Id_m}} >>>) = MAP\_Id_n$$

$$f_{ex\_h}(f_{ex\_t}(< MAP\_Id_n, < MAP\_Id_m, < MAP\_Id_j \|$$
$$MAP\_Id_i, \{MA_i\}_{prikey_{MAP\_Id_m}} >>>)) = MAP\_Id_m$$

$$f_{ex\_h}(f_{ex\_t}(f_{ex\_t}(< MAP\_Id_n, < MAP\_Id_m, < MAP\_Id_j \|$$
$$MAP\_Id_i, \{MA_i\}_{prikey_{MAP\_Id_m}} >>>))) = MAP\_Id_j \| MA\_Id_i$$

(3) Decrypting the mobile agent at the second level by using $asy(pubkey_{MAP\_Id_m}, prikey_{MAP\_Id_m}) \equiv 1$ and doing:

$$f_{dec}(f_{ex\_t}(f_{ex\_t}(f_{ex\_t}(< MAP\_Id_n, < MAP\_Id_m, < MAP\_Id_j \|$$
$$MAP\_Id_i, \{MA_i\}_{prikey_{MAP\_Id_m}} >>>))), pubkey_{MAP\_Id_m})$$
$$= MA_i$$

to get the clear-text form of mobile agent for execution.

6.4.2   *Mutual authentication between a mobile agent and a mobile agent platform*

To arrive at the belief that the right mobile agent will be executed by the right mobile agent platform, both mobile agents and mobile agent platforms have to authenticate the identity of each other. However, different from two parties in equal positions which will authenticate each other, a mobile agent is subordinate while the mobile agent platform is dominant because the mobile agent must be executed by the mobile agent platform to achieve its authentication purpose. Moreover, since a mobile agent's code, data and state may be maliciously modified by a platform which executes it and sends it out to affect other platforms, another platform which receives an incoming mobile agent also needs to identify the previous platform of this mobile agent. Therefore, we proposed the two-phase mutual authentication process as introduced below.

Firstly, a mobile agent platform authenticates the previous platform's identity and the identity of an incoming mobile agent. Recall that when a mobile agent leaves a mobile agent platform, the platform will encrypt this mobile agent using its private key; then append the destination platform identifier, the source platform identifier which should be the identifier of this platform, the identifiers pair with the encrypted mobile agent; and finally encrypts the packed mobile agent using the public key of the TS. The form of this mobile agent, after being received, checked, registered, and sent by the TS, remains the same except that it is encrypted using the public key of the destination platform. The destination platform decrypts it using its private key. But the mobile agent is still in its encrypted form under the private key of the source platform which sent it out. The destination platform can then decrypt the encrypted mobile agent using the public key of the source destination, which is also an authentication towards the source platform. We have assumed that in our system, no party can obtain private keys of other parties; and information x can only be decrypted by a key which is the asymmetric key of the encrypted key (written as $f_{dec}(f_{enc}(x,y),y') = x \Leftrightarrow asy(y,y') \equiv 1 \vee asy(y',y) \equiv 1$). So if the destination platform cannot decrypt a mobile agent correctly using the public key of the claimed source platform, it can conclude that either the mobile agent does not really come from the claimed platform, or this mobile agent coming from the claimed mobile agent platform has been attacked and modified to cause such inconsistency to happen. In either case, the destination platform may contact the TS and/or choose to ignore/discard/freeze this mobile agent to avoid any possible malicious attacks. On the contrary, if this decryption can be performed correctly, the destination platform can verify the mobile agent really comes from the claimed source platform via the TS. The encrypted mobile agent actually acts as a digital signature of the source platform in this case.

Home Platform Identifier	Mobile Agent Identifier	Commitment Time	Commitment Action

Table 10 Dangerous-party List

Next, the destination platform goes ahead to identify the mobile agent itself. This authentication is done by checking the identifiers pair of the mobile agent. When a mobile agent is created by its home platform, it is packed with an identifiers pair including its home platform identifier and its own identifier. This identifier pair is read-only and cannot be detached or modified. It is also protected to some extent by the encryption using source platform's private key because not every platform may have the corresponding public key. The destination platform maintains a "dangerous-party list" in its security base. The dangerous-party list looks like Figure 10. When the destination platform finds the identifiers pair of an incoming mobile agent in the list by searching it through the "Home Platform Identifier" and "Mobile Agent Identifier" fields, the destination platform regards this mobile agent as malicious and definitely will not risk executing it. The mobile agent will be put into the prison for special handling. A platform can choose different recognizing methods for defining a "malicious" agent according to its own security sensitiveness. For example, a platform can only look at the home platform identifier of an incoming mobile agent.

If that is found in the dangerous-party list, the mobile agent is treated as a malicious one because it is created by an identified "bad" mobile agent platform.

Secondly, if the first phase is passed successfully, the destination platform has to prove its own identity to the mobile agent. It sends a cipher-text message, which is its own identifier encrypted with its private key, to the mobile agent through internal communication channel. By that time, the mobile agent has been put into the "ready" queue of the platform and waits for being executed. Once it gets the processor of the platform, it decrypts the encrypted platform identifier using the corresponding public key of its expected destination platform. This public key is carried with the mobile agent and stored in its security base which is an internal place invisible to the outside world. Only after this decryption succeeds, that is to say, we have

$$f_{dec}(f_{enc}(MAP\_Id_i, y), pubkey_{MAP\_Id_i}) = MAP\_Id_i \Leftrightarrow$$
$$asy(pubkey_{MAP\_Id_i}, y) \equiv 1 \Leftrightarrow y = prikey_{MAP\_Id_i}$$

can the mobile agent authenticate the mobile agent platform which is going to execute it. Afterwards, the actions of this mobile agent can be activated. Reflected in Figure 23, a synchronous token can be put into place P14 to restore the execution state of this mobile agent. At the same time, the mobile agent records its current location which is this destination platform's identifier into place P4; and updates its path history by adding a new part (in the form of [Visit#, Platform-Id, Visit-Time]) at the end of the current path history. The "Visit#" is increased sequentially; the "Platform-Id" is the destination platform identifier decrypted from the platform's first message; and the "Visit-Time" is the current local time on this platform. However, if the decryption fails, that means the mobile agent arrives at a wrong platform or is intercepted by some malicious platform which cannot have the private key of the expected destination platform. Therefore, even if this mobile agent can be decrypted correctly, the actions of this mobile agent cannot be activated.

The above steps finish the mutual authentication between a mobile agent and its destination platform. If the mutual authentication goes through successfully, the mobile agent can be executed by the platform afterwards.

6.4.3   *Authorization for a mobile agent from a mobile agent platform*

After an incoming mobile agent successfully passes the authentication process of a mobile agent platform it arrives at, it will go ahead to execute on this platform and use certain resources of this platform. To protect those resources as well as legitimate accesses, the platform should be equipped with an approach to establish an authorization system. When a mobile agent tries to access some resource, the platform knows whether it should permit or deny such request in accord with the established authorizations. In order to support authorization in our system, we need to consider and solve problems from the following three aspects which are authorization expression method, authorization policy, and authorization maintenance.

6.4.3.1 *Authorization expression method*

Authorization is also called access control, which is usually expressed in terms of access rights or access modes [134]. The meaning of access rights depends on different systems. Normally, we regard all resources controlled by a computer system as objects. Various objects have various sets of access rights. For example, for a "file" object, the access rights include "Read", "Write", "Execute", "Create", and "Delete"; while for a "bank account" object, the access right include "Create", "Inquire", "Credit", "Debit", and "Cancel". Mobile agents are the only subjects we consider which can initiate activities on objects for a mobile agent platform. Conceptually, the relationships between subjects and objects are expressed by an "access matrix" which specifies the access rights that each subject possesses for each object. Each subject corresponds to a row in this matrix; each object corresponds to a column in this matrix; and the access right authorized for the subject to the object is specified by the cell corresponding to the subject row and object column. The aim of the access matrix is to ensure that only those operations authorized in this matrix can get executed for the right subjects on the right objects. A sample of access matrix is shown in Table 11.

Subjects	Object 1	Object 2	Object 3	Object 4
Mobile Agent 1	R	X	W	X
Mobile Agent 2	X	X	R	R
••••••	••••••	••••••	••••••	••••••

Table 11 A Sample Access Matrix (R – Read, W – Write, X – No Right to Access)

Since a mobile agent system may be a very large distributed system with many mobile agents and many resources of various mobile agent systems, it is neither practical nor economic to set up an access matrix for the entire system. Even if we build an individual access matrix on each mobile agent system, such matrix can still be enormous in size and probably be sparse since most of its cells are likely to be empty. Therefore, we use an alternative method to replace the access matrix in our mobile agent system.

As being introduced in section 3.3.2, there are several ways to express the access matrix differently. Access Control Lists (ACLs) correspond to storing the access matrix by columns. Capabilities correspond to storing the access matrix by rows. Authorization table corresponds to storing the access matrix by items. Because authorization table has the advantages of both ACLs and capabilities, and is more flexible than the above two, we use authorization table in our mobile agent system.

The authorization table has three columns, as illustrated in Table 12. The first one corresponds to mobile agents. Since a mobile agent is uniquely identified by its identifiers pair (HPI, SI) in the mobile agent system, each cell in the first column is an identifier pair of a certain mobile agent. The second column corresponds to resources of a mobile agent platform. Different platforms may name and define their resources differently. Without loss of generosity, here we use a "Resource_Id" to represent a certain resource. The third column shows the access rights mobile agents have for certain resources. A mobile agent platform should keep another table showing what access rights are available for each resource it has. When it authorizes a mobile agent for accessing a certain resource, and insert a row into the authorization table accordingly if that is the first time this mobile agent tries to access this resource, it must first check whether the corresponding access right requested by the mobile agent is within the set of the available access rights. If it is, the insertion is done. Otherwise, the platform will double-check what is wrong and decide what to do next.

Mobile Agent Identifiers Pair	Resource_Id	Access Right
(MAP_Id$_1$, MA_Id$_1$)	R1	R
(MAP_Id$_1$, MA_Id$_1$)	R2	X
(MAP_Id$_1$, MA_Id$_1$)	R3	W
(MAP_Id$_1$, MA_Id$_1$)	R4	X
(MAP_Id$_2$, MA_Id$_{10}$)	R1	X
(MAP_Id$_2$, MA_Id$_{10}$)	R2	X
(MAP_Id$_2$, MA_Id$_{10}$)	R3	R
(MAP_Id$_2$, MA_Id$_{10}$)	R4	R
(MAP_Id$_3$, MA_Id$_2$)	R1	W
(MAP_Id$_6$, MA_Id$_8$)	R2	X
••••••	••••••	••••••

Table 12 Authorization Table with Sample Data Sorted on Mobile Agent Identifiers Pair

Other than the authorization table method that we use in our model, there are two other main methods to represent an access matrix [134]. One is Access Control Lists (ACLs) and the other is capability lists. The former corresponds to storing the access matrix by columns. Each object has an ACL which indicates what subjects have what kinds of access rights on this object. Therefore it is convenient for access review with respect to an object or revoking all access to an object. But to determine what access rights a specific subject has, all ACLs have to be checked. On the contrary, the latter corresponds to storing the access matrix by rows. Each subject is associated with a capability list which indicates on what objects this subject has what kinds of access rights. Therefore it is convenient to review all access rights a specific subject has. But to determine what subjects have what kinds of access rights on a specific object, the capability list of each subject has to be checked. In other words, the ACLs and capability lists have dual advantages and disadvantages. Compared with these two methods, the authorization table has both advantages since it resembles ACLs when its records are sorted by objects which are Resources_Ids; while it resembles capability lists when its records are sorted by subjects which are mobile agents' identifiers pairs. Since the authorization table is also a relational table, it facilitates the database-like management of data items in a system, such as the mobile agents and platform resources in a mobile agent system.

In our EEOS model, the authorization table is stored in the security base of a mobile agent platform in the form of a special token which has table structure. Its actual data type may be different for different simulation tools. For example, we use a list of records which consist of the three fields in Table 12 to represent the authorization table in our simulation (refer to section 0).

6.4.3.2 *Authorization policy*

Authorization policies are high level guidelines which determine how accesses are controlled and how access decisions are determined [134]. Traditional authorization policies include discretionary policies and mandatory policies. Discretionary policies administer the access of subjects to objects according to the subjects' identities and the authorization rules which indicate what access rights can be granted for each subject to each object in this system. When a subject proposes a request to access a certain object, the system checks the identity of this subject against the authorization rules. If there is a rule allowing such subject to access the object, then the authorization is granted. Otherwise the authorization is denied. Although the discretionary policies are quite flexible and suitable for a variety of systems, it cannot guarantee the flow of information in a system. Mandatory policies, on the contrary, specifically define the information flow. In mandatory policies, each subject and each object is assigned a security level which reveals the trustworthiness of a subject not to disclose sensitive information and the sensitivity of the information contained in the object respectively. Then mandatory policies always define principles for information flow between security levels. When a subject tries to access an object, the mandatory policies checks whether the request satisfies certain principles defined for the security levels of the subject and the object. If it does, the authorization is granted; otherwise it is denied.

Although the two authorization policies mentioned above have been recognized in official standards, many systems and requirements are not covered by those policies. Therefore several other policies are proposed, among which the role-based authorization policies are a promising direction. A key concept in role-based policies is "role", which is a set of actions and responsibilities associated with a particular working activity. Subjects that are authorized to adopt roles and access authorizations on objects are specified for roles. A subject can take different roles on different occasions. This approach has several advantages including efficient authorization management, support for hierarchical roles, separation of duties, etc.

In our system, we proposed an authorization policy, which has the advantages of both the mandatory policy and role-based policy, called "trusted-role-based policy" or abbreviated as "TRB policy". TRB policy also defines a set of roles which are actions associated with a particular activity. On the one hand, subjects, which are mobile agents in our system, can request roles based on their goals after they are authenticated. A mobile agent can request different roles on different mobile agent systems and on the same mobile agent system at different times. But at any one time, a mobile agent can only take on one role. To set up a role for a mobile agent, a mobile agent platform has to ask for some credible information from that agent. By checking the information provided by the mobile agent, the mobile agent platform assigns a trust level to that mobile agent. And then the mobile agent platform inserts the corresponding role and trust level values into the entry for this mobile agent in the registration table. The trust level indicates the trustworthiness of this mobile agent requesting that role and will be used by this platform together with its role to determine which accesses should be authorized to a mobile agent. The highest level trusted-role corresponds to all defined actions and responsibilities of that role, while a lower level trusted-role only corresponds to a subset of those predefined actions and responsibilities. Trusted-roles at different levels may correspond to the same set of actions on certain objects. On the other hand, the information flow concerning resources between mobile agents (should be through the mobile agent platform they reside on) can only be from the mobile agents with lower trust level to mobile agents with higher trust levels or between mobile agents on the same trust level, no matter what roles they take on. This is to prevent leaking of information of the platform. There is no need for us to define a trust level for objects, which are platform resources, in our policy for ensuring information flow because the access rights for objects are specified with each role.

We will use an example of a simplified electronic airline-ticket booking mobile agent system to solidify our TRB policy. In the system, mobile agents are roaming among a set of mobile agent platforms which offer airline tickets. The roles that a mobile agent can take on include "Inquirer", "Customer", and "Agent". The platform resources mainly include the following database tables:

airline-company (company name, address, contact information, safety rate),

airline(company name, flight number, departure city, arrival city, departure time, arrival time, plane type),

ticket (company name, flight number, departure time, class, price, availability),

customer (customer name, identification number, category),

agent (agent name, contact information, paying method, reputation),

booking (customer name, company name, flight number, cost, class, agent).

The predefined complete actions of these three roles may look like the following (where R means Read, W means Write, R(x) means the subject has the Read right on table x, $R_l(x)$ means the subject has the

Read right on only one line corresponding to itself on table x, R_s (x) means the subject has the Read right on a set of rows corresponding to itself on table x):

ACT *(Inquirer(i))* $=\{R$ *(airline-company), R (airline), R (ticket)}*;
ACT *(Customer(i))* $=\{R$ *(airline-company), R (airline), R (ticket), $R_l W_l$ (Customer), $R_s W_s$ (booking)}*;
ACT *(Agent(i))* $= \{R$ *(airline-company), R (airline), R (ticket), RW (customer), $R_l W_l$ (agent), $R_s W_s$ (booking)}*;

The trusted level may include "3-Confidential", "2-Average" and "1-Default". Since the highest level trusted-role corresponds to all defined actions of that role, we have

$ACT(x, 3) = ACT(x)$ *(x= Inquirer, Customer, or Agent)*

The actions set for lower level trusted-roles may look like the following (where just one possibility is shown):

ACT *(Inquirer, 2)* $=\{R$ *(airline-company), R (airline)}*;
ACT *(Inquirer, 1)* $=\{R$ *(airline-company)}*;
ACT *(Customer, 2)* $=\{R$ *(airline-company), R (airline), R (ticket), R_l (Customer), R_s (booking)}*;
ACT *(Customer, 1)* $=\{R$ *(airline-company), R (airline), R (ticket)}*;
ACT *(Agent, 2)* $= \{R$ *(airline-company), R (airline), R (ticket), R (customer), R_l (agent),R_s (booking)}*;
ACT *(Agent, 1)* $= \{R$ *(airline-company), R (airline), R (ticket)}*;

Suppose that two mobile agents MA1, MA2 arrive at a mobile agent platform offering airline tickets and MA1 requests an "Agent" role while MA requests a "Customer" role. The platform will ask for their user names and passwords. The user name of a mobile agent is not the identifiers pair of this agent used for authentication, but the user name is also unique in this system. Suppose this is the first time that MA1 visited this platform, it tells the platform that it wants to register for a new agent on behalf of its owner. Then the platform asks for some more information, e.g.,   its owner's name, contact information, payment method such as credit card information, etc. MA1 presents the information to the platform for its check. If all information is correct, the platform may register this user account, set up its password based on MA1's choice, and assign a highest level trusted-role to MA1. MA1 can begin its execution in accordance with the access rights associated with ACT (Agent, 3). For MA2, suppose it has visited the platform and registered before, then MA2 replies the platform's request with its user name and password. They match the record for travel agents in the platform's knowledge base. But MA2 may come from a source platform which is totally strange to this platform, the platform may just assign a second level trusted-role to MA2 in case this source platform is a malicious one and takes advantage of MA2 to do some bad things. In this case, MA2 can only do the accesses allowed by ACT (Customer, 2). Suppose MA1 and MA2 are aware of each other's existence in this platform and want to communicate with each other. According to their trusted-role levels, any information related to the contents of those database files can only flow from MA2 to MA1. For instance, if MA2 asks MA1 to send some information related to the agent table to it, such request will be denied because the MA2's trust level is lower than MA1's.

The concrete rules for defining action sets for roles, determining which level of trust should be assigned to a mobile agent, and controlling the information flow among mobile agents with different roles and different trust levels should be decided by individual mobile agent systems because they have various requirements in various applications.

6.4.3.3 *Authorization maintenance*

Once a mobile agent has been assigned a trusted-role, the platform inserts lines into the authorization table corresponding to this mobile agent and certain resources. Any attempt of this mobile agent to any resource will be checked based on the authorization table. The authorization table contents vary from time to time. A platform does not need to store the entries for a specific mobile agent once it leaves the platform, because each time the mobile agent visits the platform, the trusted-roles of that mobile agent may be different hence the access rights for it may be different. So the platform eliminates the entries corresponding to the mobile agent when it dispatches the mobile agent to the network. This can also help with reducing the space needed to store the authorization table on that platform.

A mobile agent platform needs to store and maintain the actions for different trusted-roles in a role action table. This table can be realized by using the similar structure to access matrix, ACL, or capability list. If a mobile agent platform has some new resources to service mobile agents, it will update the role action table and add certain access rights to these new resources for trusted-roles. It will delete certain cells if some existing resources are not available any more. It can also create new roles for incoming mobile agents to take. How these can be determined rely heavily on different applications.

6.4.4   *Data security and action security*

After a mobile agent passes mutual authentication and is authorized based on its trusted-role, it is put into the ready queue of the platform waiting to be executed. Secure execution of a mobile agent on a mobile agent platform involved two aspects. On the one hand, executing the mobile agent should not affect the normal functionalities of the mobile agent platform and other programs running on the same computer. On the other hand, the mobile agent should be executed correctly and securely by the platform. The former aspect aims to protect a mobile agent platform from possible attacks of a malicious mobile agent. As introduced in section 4.1.1.2 and section 4.2.2.1, problems in this category have been encountered in the traditional client-server environment and dealt with using techniques used to protect servers in the traditional distributed system. While the latter concerns protecting a mobile agent from the malicious platforms. This aspect is seldom met before and remains a challenging area. In our model, we are concerned with both data security and action security during a mobile agent's execution. Before we start discussing these two aspects, it should be noted that a mobile agent platform to execute a mobile agent is not really the operating system platform or certain virtual machine environment which actually interprets and executes the mobile agent, but just a software program running on the operating system or virtual machine which can manage mobile agents. Therefore, although a mobile agent platform can interfere with a mobile agent's execution to a great extent, it cannot change the normal behaviors or predefined principles of the operating system or virtual machine to accomplish its malicious attacks. This is the basic assumption for our mechanisms towards mobile agent's data security and action security.

6.4.4.1 *Data security*

A mobile agent carries different data with it during its travel, such as its identifiers pair, its knowledge, etc. Some of the data must be exposed to a mobile agent platform for the normal execution of this mobile agent on this platform, while some are not needed for the specific execution. For the latter, we need data hiding to achieve data security.

The "internal places" we proposed in section 5.3.2.4 provides a mechanism for information hiding. Due to the invisibility of an internal place, tokens in an internal place should also be invisible to the outside world. Therefore, any outside entity does not have the ability to access or update such tokens. In our model, the knowledge base of a mobile agent, which stores the data and other information obtained by this mobile agent, is declared as an internal place whose state can only be changed by internal transitions linked to the knowledge base. When a mobile agent gets executed in a mobile agent platform, it exchanges data with this platform through its communication channels. The platform cannot directly change the data inside the knowledge base of a mobile agent.

Such internal places can be implemented, for example, by defining data members as "private" in a C++ or Java program. Any attempt to access or modify such data members by other object instances would be denied because it is the principle of C++ or Java that only the member functions or methods of the same object instance are allowed to do so.

6.4.4.2 *Action security*

We propose a security mechanism to detect possible attacks to mobile agent's code or mobile agent execution flow, which is called "synchronous firing security mechanism". Simply put, with respect to the execution of a mobile agent's code, the consequences of possible attacks to it can be classified into two kinds of errors: the mobile agent did NOT do what it should have done, or it did what it should NOT have done. We can view the former as some part of the mobile agent code has been omitted or removed. A malicious mobile agent platform can deliberately jump over that code segment by controlling the execution sequence, or actually delete that part of code to achieve this goal. No matter which way a malicious platform acts, corresponding code segments of the mobile agent will be ignored during its execution. Viewed from the modeling aspect, the EEOS structure of that mobile agent is definitely changed. The synchronous firing security mechanism is designed to detect attacks belonging to this category.

In the synchronous firing mechanism, the object net in the security mechanism layer (``S-net'' for simplicity) has the similar structure and content as the mobile agent system net (``M-net'' for simplicity). Each transition in the S-net has the extended interaction relation with the corresponding transition in the M-net. The differences between an S-net and its corresponding M-net are listed below. Firstly, the Security Base place in the M-net is absent in the S-net. Secondly, an additional "Firing Log" place, which records the firing sequence of transitions, is added into the S-net. Thirdly, S-net is encrypted. Each transition in S-net is encrypted separately. At the same time, each transition in the M-net has a special extended interaction relation with its corresponding counterpart transition in S-net. The former is responsible to decrypt the latter when a mobile agent is executed. The first two differences are easy to understand. An S-net is not equipped with further security protection because it has been encrypted, so a Security Base is not needed in an S-net. Firing of transitions in an S-net is recorded in its Firing Log place for later checking by the home platform of the mobile agent carrying the S-net. The third is the key point of this mechanism and we will discuss it in more detail.

Recall that in our EEOS, extended interaction relation, between a pair of transitions in a system net and an object net, makes one transition in this pair be fired right before the firing of the other transition. The one which fires first is called "driving transition" and the one which fires later is called "driven transition" (refer to section 5.3.2.6). In the synchronous firing mechanism, the special extended interaction relation between a driving transition in M-net and a driven transition in S-net is a decryption relation. That is, a driving transition in M-net is responsible for decrypting its counterpart driven transition, which is in its encrypted form in S-net. The decryption algorithm is integrated in the driving transition in the M-net. Once a transition in M-net is fired, the decryption part gets activated and decrypts the corresponding driven transition in the S-net. The driven transition in the S-net, which has the same enabling conditions as its driving transition in the M-net except for the extended interaction relation, is enabled as well and may get fired. Reflected to the real world, transitions represent code in a mobile agent. Therefore, after decryption, executable code corresponding to the driven transition is acquired. It is then stored in certain areas within the memory of the executing machine on which the mobile agent platform runs. Afterwards, the code is executed and appropriate execution information is inserted into a firing record carried with the mobile agent. After execution, this segment of code may remove itself from the memory. Reflected in the EEOS model, when the driven transition of the S-net is fired, the firing information is added as a token into the Firing Log place of the S-net. Then the driven transition is disabled. After a mobile agent finishes its execution on a guest platform and returns to its home platform (the ``single-hop'' situation is considered here for simplicity), the home platform checks the result it brings back, its state, together with the Firing-Log content of its S-net. If the former is not in correspondence with the latter, then the home platform can conclude that the mobile agent might have been attacked by the guest platform or some third party. And the home platform can check the Firing-Log contents further to reveal when the attack happened and what the attacks could be. We use a simple example to illustrate this mechanism in the following.

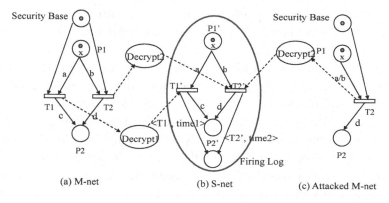

(a) M-net   (b) S-net   (c) Attacked M-net

Figure 30 An Example of Synchronous Firing Mechanism

In the following example illustrated in Figure 30, (a) is the original M-net; (b) is the corresponding S-net; and (c) is the M-net after being attacked.

In (a), an M-net consists of two places P1, P2, two transitions T1, T2, plus a security base place. According to the marking on different arcs and the initial token type in place P1, different transitions will be fired and a different token will be put in P2. In (b), the corresponding S-net structure is similar to the M-net in (a) with the three changes mentioned above. Initially, the token in Place P1 is with value $x = a$. If the platform is trustable, T1 will be fired and P2 will get a token with type c. If the M-net has NOT been attacked at all, firing T1 decrypts transition T1' in the S-net. As a result, P2' in the S-net also holds token c and the Firing Log holds a firing record <T1', time1> (suppose T1' is fired in time1). However, suppose the mobile agent has been attacked. No matter which type of the token is in place P1, only transition T2 fires and token d is added into place P2. In this case, the T1 part of the M-net is removed and the attacked M-net is shown in (c). In this case, firing T2 in the attacked M-net will decrypt transition T2' in the S-net, rather than T1'. But since the token type $x = a$, transition T2' is not fired in S-net. T1' is not fired either since it has not been decrypted yet. As a result, the Firing Log does not have any firing record and the place P2' does not hold any token. Therefore, after the mobile agent with its S-net returns to the home platform, the home platform can detect the discrepancy between the M-net state and the S-net state. Thus, the attack to the mobile agent could be detected.

For this synchronous firing security mechanism, we discuss several questions below. Firstly, it should be aware that even being encrypted, the S-net still has the possibility of being attacked. But the possibility is really low for an encrypted program which has been attacked and modified to be executed correctly after being decrypted. And the possibility is even lower that both the attacked M-net and attacked S-net have the consistent results that can deceive the home platform. Secondly, one may worry that a malicious platform might try to change the S-net part after it has been decrypted by firing the corresponding M-net part. We think that the following features of our mechanism can help with decreasing such possibility. Our security mechanism only allows a transition in S-net to be decrypted right after its corresponding transition in M-net is fired. The time spent on an individual decryption and execution of a transition is not long, and after the execution, the decrypted version of the transition in S-net will be removed by itself. During such short period, a malicious platform does not have much chance to carry out its plot. Thirdly, if the malicious platform knows how to decrypt a transition in the S-net, will it be able to decrypt all other transitions in S-net without firing the M-net? To give a negative answer, we may use different encryption methods for different transitions in S-net, or use different keys embedded in the corresponding driving transitions in the M-net so that only firing them can decrypt the driven transitions in S-net. Therefore, the synchronous security mechanism can improve the security level for a mobile agent from the detection point of view.

It should be mentioned that the synchronous firing mechanism in the EEOS is expressed as a token carried with the mobile agent object net. This token has its detailed structure visible in the top layer of a mobile agent system, which is the security mechanism layer. Petri nets in this layer are object nets of system nets representing mobile agents in mobile agent layer. They are carried by mobile agents as tokens. Since there might be different security mechanisms, the structures of token nets in this layer are not fixed. More security mechanisms can be added to this layer to support security for the generic mobile agent system from different aspects.

Chapter 7

Translating the EEOS Model to Colored Petri Net Model

Petri Nets, as a graphical formal method, is also a simulation tool for a system under study. Simulation and simulation-based analysis provide a thorough view of the behaviors and characteristics of a system. Since our EEOS stems from CPN, we simulate our EEOS model for a generic secure mobile agent system in Design/CPN, the most widely used package for CPN. Before simulation, we need to translate our EEOS model to CPN model supported by Design/CPN.

The following problems should be addressed during the translation. First, tokens in an ordinary CPN only have colors, no structures. But in our EEOS, a token can be a Petri net as well as a colored token. How to represent an object net in CPN becomes the most important issue in our translation. Second, dynamic connection is required for the communication between mobile agent and mobile agent platform. But a CPN model in Design/CPN has fixed structure. Therefore, we need a method to realize the conditioned transition proposed in our EEOS model. Third, the two new arcs we introduced into EEOS for simplifying conceptual modeling should be translated to ordinary CPN structures for the model to be able to simulate. Fourth, concerning the information declaration such as communication message format declaration, we must adapt appropriate CPN data type declarations. These four aspects are the main concerns when we translate our EEOS model to CPN model and will be discussed in detail in the following sections.

7.1 Object Net Tokens and Special Tokens

7.1.1 *Object net tokens*

Simply speaking, our method to address the object token net problem is to separate the views. Viewed from the mobile agent platform system net, a mobile agent token net is just like an ordinary token. It can be moved from one place to another, which indicates different stages the mobile agent is in during the processing, by firing certain transitions in the platform system net. Viewed from the mobile agent object net, it has its own structure and behaviors which are modeled in the mobile agent level. Therefore, in the CPN model, a mobile agent object net should have both. In our CPN model, a mobile agent platform system net and a mobile agent object net are modeled respectively on different pages. They are related together by assigning "critical tokens" to these two net models to coordinate their activities. Here critical tokens refer to those tokens which can enable the activities of object nets or identify the existence of an object net to a system net.

Suppose we are to model a generic mobile agent system with two mobile agent platform Plat1 and Plat2, and two mobile agents MA1 and MA10. Conceptually, MA1 is created by Plat1 and MA10 is created by Plat2. Both mobile agents can travel within the network consisting of two mobile agent platforms. We can first come up with the static structures of the CPN models for these four components separately based on our generic models for mobile agent and mobile agent platform, then put informational tokens into four static structures respectively, such as data tokens and identifier token carried in Knowledge Base. At this point, mobile agent platforms Plat1 and Plat2 should have the ability to do some activities, but mobile agents MA1 and MA10 haven't because they are not yet "created" by the mobile agent platforms. It's like a class corresponding to mobile agents has not been instantiated. To model the creation of a mobile agent by a mobile agent platform, a special token with reference to the mobile agent object net, which is called "mobile agent style token", is generated by certain transition of the mobile agent platform model. At the same time, the mobile agent's activities should be correspondingly enabled by placing certain critical token to the mobile agent's net model based on the location of the mobile agent style token in the platform model. To a mobile agent object net, "critical token" refers to the synchronous token in place P5. Only after P5 of a mobile agent holds a synchronous token (its bound = 1 for synchronization purpose) can the activities of this mobile agent be enabled. In this way, a mobile agent token net is bounded to a mobile agent platform system net.

For mobile agent execution, we also need to take care of the two parts simultaneously. To a mobile agent platform, only after a mobile agent style token is put into place P6 (ready queue) can the mobile agent represented by the style token be executed by this mobile agent platform. Once the mobile agent is assigned the processor and gets executed, the style token of this mobile agent will be in the place Executing and transition Executes should be fired from time to time which takes and returns mobile agent style token to place Executing in the mobile agent platform model, as illustrated in Figure 19. Meanwhile for the mobile agent, certain actions including reactive action, autonomous action and move action can be performed sequentially or in parallel under the control of the synchronous token.

Once the mobile agent executes a move action, no matter if this is an active move or a negative move, its execution should terminate. From the mobile agent side, its move action takes off the synchronous token from place P5, which causes its execution to terminate. Therefore, other actions of it get halted and it is in the state of waiting to leave or leaving. From the mobile agent platform side, the mobile agent style token is moved to place P8. Next the mobile agent token is encrypted by transition T9, then put to place P2 (external out-going channel). The mobile agent style token is able to migrate to the other mobile agent platform via the token pool. But the activities in its corresponding object net are disabled until the style token arrives at the other platform. The style token has to pass the authentication and authorization to be placed to p6 in another mobile agent platform model to wait for execution.

Compared to the method that a mobile agent and its platform are on the same level net structure and connected by a location place proposed by some researchers, our method more naturally and accurately captures the features of a mobile agent execution and migration, and embodies the concepts of object better by encapsulating the details of a mobile agent structure and behaviors inside its object net while the mobile agent platform only knows its outside ports for communication and execution. In addition, Design/CPN supports hierarchy techniques, which allow a CPN to be kept on multiple pages that can be organized into a functioning whole, much as an ordinary program can be written as multiple modules that can be linked into an executable file. We take advantage of this hierarchy technique not only for the relationship between mobile agents and mobile agent platforms, but also for refining certain transitions for both. Therefore, we can change the structure or behavior of some part without changing its outside world as long as the in/out ports remain the same. That characteristic equips the model with much flexibility and extendibility. In our current model, we assume that once a mobile agent finishes its execution, it proceeds to migrate. And we ignore different situations not directly related to mobile agent, like processes competing for processor. With the feature mentioned above, it is relatively easier for our model to integrate different situations into it.

7.1.2 *Special tokens*

In our EEOS model, some data structures are required to achieve the security goals and other goals. For example, the authorization table is needed for a mobile agent platform to grant authorizations to visiting mobile agents. Such a data structure is easy to implement for some programming languages, such as using a multidimensional array or a linked list in C++. But such programming language is hard to be incorporated into Design/CPN and we have to use the data types supported in Design/CPN to realize such data structure. Table 13 is part of the global declaration of data structure for the authorization mechanism. Other data structure can be defined similarly.

```
(* Colorsets for authorization mechanism *)
color role_type = with role1 | rot2 | role3;
color trust_level = index tstlv with 1..10;
color TRB_record = product identifiers_pair * role_type * trust_level;
color TRB = list TRB_record;
```

color *access_type* = *index accty with 1..10;*
color *resource* = *with res1 | res2 | res3;*
color *authorize_table_record* = *produce identifiers_pair* * *resource* *
access_type;
color *authorize_table* – *list authorize_table_record;*

Table 13 Part of the global declaration for authorization mechanism

7.2   Dynamic Connection

As introduced in section 6.2.1, since the static structure of EEOS cannot
change, statically complete connection and exclusively conditioned
transitions are proposed to realize the dynamic connection between
mobile agents and mobile agent platforms. Statically complete
connection is built between each mobile agent and each mobile agent
platform when they are modeled. While for translating the "exclusively
conditioned transitions" into CPN model in Design/CPN, we need to
use the guard and code segment of a transition supported by
Design/CPN. A guard is actually a condition statement associated with a
transition. When it evaluates to TRUE, the corresponding transition gets
fired and otherwise if it is FALSE. When a transition is fired, its code
segment gets executed, which may perform certain computation on the
input values and set different output values.

As for the realization of the exclusively conditioned transitions to
achieve dynamic connection between mobile agents and mobile agent
platforms, in the guard of the transition connecting this mobile agent
and an expected mobile agent platform, we need to check the current
location of the mobile agent under consideration and also check whether
the mobile agent is in the mobile agent platform's visiting mobile agent
lists. Only when these conditions related to the location of this mobile
agent are satisfied (and other restricting conditions are satisfied such as
this mobile agent is not a NULL), will the connecting transition be
enabled. These two conditions related to a mobile agent's location seem
redundant but actually not, because they are from different views from a
mobile agent and a mobile agent platform respectively. Normally if a
mobile agent's location indicates that this mobile agent is on a mobile
agent platform, the corresponding mobile agent platform's visiting

mobile agent list should contain this mobile agent. But the possibility exists that the mobile agent's location and the platform's visiting mobile agent list are attacked maliciously and not consistent. Therefore, including both into the guard increases the assurance level that this mobile agent really resides on this mobile agent platform. After the guard conditions are met, the connecting transition gets fired and the code segment of this transition then "transports" the communicating messages from this mobile agent to this mobile agent platform or vice versa. By writing different guards for transitions in the complete communication connections between mobile agents and mobile agent platforms, appropriate transition should be dynamically enabled and fired based on different markings of the entire system model; and thus controls the communication flow dynamically.

The following examples realize the dynamic connection for the mobile agent system shown in Figure 24 (a) for the communication from mobile agents Ma1, Ma2 to mobile agent platforms P1 and P2. For any mobile agent, say Ma1, its location is unique at any time. Therefore, at most one of the transitions Ma1_P1 and Ma2_P2, which are a pair of exclusively conditioned transitions, can be enabled and fired.

Transition	Guard	Code Segment
Ma1_P1	[Ma1_loc=P1, Has(P1_Ma,Ma1)=1, Ma1<>NULL]	Input(Ma1); Output(Ma1_in); Action{Ma1_in= Ma1;}
Ma1_P2	[Ma1_loc=P2, Has(P2_Ma,Ma1)=1, Ma1<>NULL]	Input(Ma1); Output(Ma1_in); Action{Ma1_in= Ma1;}
Ma2_P1	[Ma2_loc=P1, Has(P1_Ma,Ma2)=1, Ma2<>NULL]	Input(Ma2); Output(Ma2_in); Action{Ma2_in= Ma2;}
Ma2_P2	[Ma2_loc=P1, Has(P2_Ma,Ma2)=1, Ma2<>NULL]	Input(Ma2); Output(Ma2_in); Action{Ma2_in= Ma2;}

Table 14 Guards and Code Segments for Exclusively Conditioned Transitions

7.3   New Constructs – Two New Arcs and Extended Interaction Relation

7.3.1 *Two new arcs*

With respect to the two new arcs we introduced into EEOS, we can take advantage of the existing CPN components to express them. The update arc can be simply represented by two arcs with labels different from each other or the same as each other.

Figure 31 Figure 31 shows a simple example of realizing an update arc where the guard of the corresponding transition tests whether there is a non-null token in place P, and the code segment accomplishes the computation of the output token based on the input token of this transition. The relationship between the input token a and output token b is expressed using a function b = f(a). When f(x) = x, the input token and output token are the same and the update arc acts as a test arc.

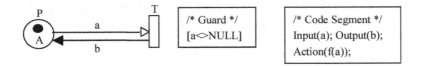

Figure 31 Realization of Update Arc

The differ-remove arc can be represented by some structure similar to what we introduced in Figure 12 (2). We can also utilize the code segment of a transition connecting to a differ-remove arc to differentiate the behaviors of this transition under different situations. Since for different transitions, the method used in dealing with such arc is not quite the same, we would not include all the details here.

7.3.2 *Extended interaction relation*

In our EEOS model (refer to section 5.3.2.6), extended interaction relation is between a pair of transitions, one of which is the driving transition and the other is the driven transition. The firing of driving transition is one of the conditions for enabling the corresponding driven transition. And if the driven transition is also enabled after firing its driving transition, it should be fired right after.

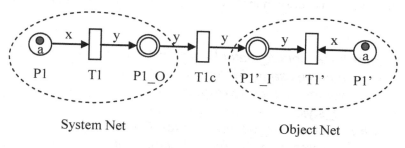

System Net   Object Net

Figure 32 Realization of the Extended Interaction Relation

Figure 32 shows a simplified example of realizing the extended interaction relation between driving transition T1 in system net and driven transition T1' in object net. Places P1_O and P1'_I are two external places added to the system net and object net respectively which are connected by the connecting transition T1c. Adding these two external places and connecting transition is to abide by the principle that T1 and T1' are internal transitions and can only connect to places belonging to the same semantic net. Suppose the guard of T1 is [True] which means as long as P1 holds certain token T1 is enabled. Then the guard of T1' would also be [True] which means as long as P1' and P1'_I ($|\bullet T1'| = \{P1', P1'\_I\}$) hold certain tokens, T1' is enabled. T1c's guard is also [True]. Now P1 and P1' both hold token a. Then T1 is enabled and fired, which generates token y into P1_O and enables transition T1c in turn. T1c's firing generates token y into place P1'_I. And therefore T1' is also enabled and gets fired. To guarantee that any transition which is enabled can get fired as soon as possible, we should select the 100% concurrency when the model is simulated.

7.4   Complicated Communication

Regarding the last aspect for data type declaration, we mainly used the compound colorset declarations supported by Design/CPN which include index, list, record, product and union. These types combined together enable the expression of complicated information type. For example, we use the following declarations for the internal communications between mobile agents and mobile agent platforms.

......

color base_comm_matopl = **union** Message:
    basemessage_fromma + Data : data;
color comm_matopl = **product** mobileagent * platform *
    m_style * base_comm_matopl;
color base_comm_pltoma = **union** Comm :
    basemessage_frompl + PDate : data;
color base_comm_ptm = **product** mobileagent *
    base_comm_pltoma;
color comm_ptm = **product** platform * base_comm_ptm;
color comm_pltoma = **union** Encrypt_pid : encryptpid_toma
    + Info : comm_ptm;

......

Chapter 8

Simulation and Analysis of the Extended Elementary Object System Model of a Secure Mobile Agent System

Simulation and simulation-based analysis provide a thorough view of the system behaviors and characteristics. Since our EEOS stems from CPN, we simulated our sample EEOS model of a generic secure mobile agent system in Design/CPN, the most widely used package for CPN. We use Design/CPN 4.0 for Solaris on a Sun Workstation. Figure 33 shows the page hierarchy of the model exported from Design/CPN.

Simulation in Design/CPN can be performed either interactively or automatically. The former gives us a more intuitive impression about the behaviors of the model while the latter can support powerful analysis tools based on the occurrence graph or reachability graph. These tools not only provide the embedded standard analysis for boundedness, liveness, etc., but also support user-defined analysis.

It should be noted that with different initial markings, system behaviors could be quite different. In our sample simulation model, there are two mobile agents (Ma1 and Ma10), the trust server (TS) and two mobile agent platforms (Plat1 and Plat2). Ma1 and Ma10 are created by Plat1 and Plat2 respectively. They will travel to the other platforms other than their home platforms to acquire some data and then go back to their home platforms. Two mobile agent platforms are responsible for administrating those two mobile agents in their life spans. After the two mobile agents come back to their own home platforms and report the data acquired respectively, activities of this system are accomplished and then the system halts.

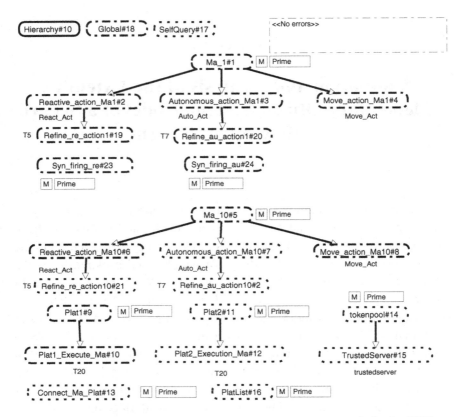

Figure 33 Page Hierarchy of the Model for a Mobile Agent System in Design/CPN

Table 15 is part of the standard simulation report generated by Design/CPN after the simulation of the sample system model is complete. It includes the statistics and a small part of the properties results of this model obtained from calculation and analysis of its OCC graph.

Statistics

Occurrence Graph
    Nodes: 42184
    Arcs: 121096

Secs: 300
Status: Partial

Boundedness Properties

Best Integers Bounds	Upper	Lower
....		
Move_action_ma1'P10 1	1	0
Move_action_ma10'P10 1	1	0
....		
plat1'Pmarec 1	2	0
plat2'Pmarec 1	2	0
....		

Best Upper Multi-set Bounds

....	
Move_action_ma1'P10 1	1`waiting
Move_action_ma10'P10 1	1`waiting
....	
Plat1'P_marec 1	1`((1,1),ma(1))++ 1`((2,10),ma(10))
Plat2'P_marec 1	1`((1,1),ma(1))++ 1`((2,10),ma(10))
....	

Best Lower Multi-set Bounds

....	
Move_action_ma1'P10 1	empty
Move_action_ma10'P10 1	empty
....	
Plat1'P_marec 1	empty
Plat2'P_marec 1	empty
....	

Liveness Properties

Dead Markings: 1131 [42184,42183,42182,42181,42180,...]

Table 15 Statistic and Properties of the Model in Design/CPN

Based on our simulation, we can perform two kinds of analysis. The first kind of analysis can be supported directly from the standard simulation report generated by Design/CPN, which includes Reachability properties, Boundedness properties and Liveness Properties. The advantage of this analysis is that usually it is easy and conclusion of features can be drawn more obviously. But the drawback is that it can only support some generic analysis and some complex analysis cannot be done in this way. The second kind of analysis is performed based on user-defined queries about the Occurrence Graph, which is the state space, of the model. Although such queries are always complicated and not easy to write, they can provide more insights into the model and support analysis for ad-hoc features, such as security features. For simplicity, we call the first kind of analysis as "standard analysis" and the second as "query-based analysis".

Standard analysis is mainly based on the standard simulation report directly generated by Design/CPN. It is not practical to post all content of this report in this paper. Therefore, we only abstract a small part of the content which we interested in to Table 15. From it, we can prove several features of the sample mobile agent system. To formalize the features that simulation-based analysis can support, we introduce the formalisms in Table 16.

Formalisms	Meanings
$MA_i \rightarrow MAP_j$	a mobile agent MA_i is traveling to a platform MAP_j
$MA_i \infty MAP_j$	a mobile agent is MA_i on a platform MAP_j
$MAP_j = Home(MA_i)$	platform MAP_j is the home platform for mobile agent MA_i
$@[t1, t2]$ $@t$	during the time interval [t1, t2] (including t1 and t2) at the time point t
$\|MA_i\|$ $\|\sum MA_k\| \ (k = 1, ..., m)$	number of mobile agents MA_i (satisfy certain conditions) the total number of mobile agents in the system
$Comm(MA_i, MAP_j)$	mobile agent MA_i can communicate with platform MAP_j
$Exec(MA_i, MAP_j)$ $Supervised(MA_i, MAP_j)$	mobile agent MA_i is executed by platform MAP_j mobile agent MA_i is supervised by platform MAP_j
$\{\}$	enclosed conditions
$x \ In \ y$	x is an element of y
$MAX(x)$	Maximum value of x

Table 16 Formalisms to Express Mobile Agent System Features

8.1 Reachability

Recall that in our sample model used for the simulation, two mobile agents intend to request some data which they don't have from some mobile agent platform. Whether they can get those expected data could be checked using the reachability properties.

Feature 1. $\exists i,j,t\,(MA_i \infty MAP_j \,@\,t \wedge MAP_j = Home(MA_i) \wedge Data(x)\,in\,MA_i$.

Explanation: This formula states that at some time, a mobile agent can go back to its home platform with the data they are asked to obtain

Proof: To prove this feature, we wrote the following query function in CPN ML:

```
fun aquiredata(x1,x2:data, y1,y2:packed_ma): bool =
(PredAllNodes(fn n=>((Cf(x1, Mark.Ma_1'P8 1 n)>0
                andalso
                Cf(y1, Mark.Plat1'P81 n) >0)
                andalso
                (Cf(x2, Mark.Ma_2'P8 1 n)>0
                andalso
                Cf(y2, Mark.Plat2'P81 n) >0))<>[]);
```

This function evaluates whether it is true that two data items x1, x2 could be finally obtained in Ma_1 and Ma_2, which are two mobile agents on their home platform Plat1 and Plat2 respectively. It evaluates to TRUE in the reachability graph when x1 and x2 are replaced by the data items two mobile agents expect to get.

8.2 Boundedness

We can prove the following two features of the sample mobile agent system by checking the boundedness properties of the sample model.

Feature 2.

$\forall i,j,k,t,(MA_i \rightarrow MAP_j \parallel MA_i \rightarrow TS)\,@ \Leftrightarrow \neg(MA_i \infty MAP_k \,@\,t)\ \{k=1,...,n\}$

Explanation: This formula states that at any time, a mobile agent MA_i either travels to a mobile agent platform, or travels to the trust server, or resides on one of n mobile agent platforms. This feature guarantees the single destination of one move of a mobile agent. A mobile agent cannot be transferred to more than one destination simultaneously, which is a basic requirement of a mobile agent system. Only after this requirement is meet, can the location of a mobile agent be meaningful. It needs to be pointed out that the agent cloning is not considered in our system.

Proof: This feature is from standard analysis by checking the boundedness properties of the moving state indicator P10 and current location P4 for mobile agents. The upper bound of those places is equal to 1 and the lower bound is 0. The upper bound of P10 is 1 means at any time, a mobile agent can have up to one move action to one platform performed. The upper bound of P4 is 1 means at any time, a mobile agent can be residing on up to one platform. While by checking the simulation result, the upper bounds of P10 and P4 cannot be reached simultaneously, but at least one of them should be present. Therefore we can come to the above conclusion.

Feature 3. $\forall i, j, k, t, MA_i \infty MAP_j @ t \Rightarrow |MA_i| \leq Max(|MA_k|)$

Explanation: This formula states that at any time, a mobile agent platform can only hold up to the maximum numbers of mobile agents created in the entire system. This feature guarantees that the number of mobile agents in the sample system cannot exceed the number of mobile agents created by mobile agent platforms. Therefore, a mobile agent cannot get cloned during its transportation process. This feature prevents a malicious mobile agent platform, which might hide from visibility of the entire system, from cloning some mobile agents on their way to other trustworthy platforms and modifying the clones afterwards to fulfill their own goals.

Proof: This feature is also proven by the boundedness properties of the place of each mobile agent platform which records the mobile agents residing on it. The upper bound of such places for both Plat1 and Plat2 is equal to 2, which is the maximum number of the mobile agents created in the entire sample system.

8.3   Liveness

The following features can be proved by checking the liveness properties of the sample model.

Feature 4.

$\forall i, \exists j, t, MA_i \infty MAP_j @ t \wedge \neg(MA_i \infty MAP_k @ [t+1, t1])\{MAP_j = Home(MA_i), t1 > t+1\}$

Explanation: This formula states that a mobile agent should be able to finish its migration and return to its home platform. This feature prevents the endless journey of a mobile agent. It also shows that in the sample secure mobile agent system model, a mobile agent is not subject to the attack that keeps it waiting endlessly due to the Denial-of-Service attack. It also guarantees that a home platform should be able to get back the mobile agents it creates.

Proof: This feature is proven by the liveness properties and the assumption of the sample system that the system halts after mobile agents accomplished their tasks and return to their home platforms. By tracking the dead markings, we can prove that they are reached after every mobile agent returns to its home platform after its journey. Therefore, this kind of "deadlock" is what we desired.

The three features we defined, proved and explained above are a sample set of standard analysis that we can do in Design/CPN environment. More such analysis can be continued by investigating more into the standard report. Besides the standard analysis, we can also investigate some advanced characteristics of this system model by using user-defined CPN ML functions to probe and query the Occurrence Graph of the model. We are listing some of the results below.

8.4   Concurrency

For a mobile agent system containing multiple mobile agents and mobile agent systems, the concurrency remains an important issue to be considered. Simulation-based analysis shows that our system model supports concurrency.

Feature 5. $\exists t, i1, i2, MA_{i1} \rightarrow MAP_{j1} @ t \wedge MA_{i2} \rightarrow MAP_{j2} @ t$

Explanation: This formula states that two mobile agents can travel at the same time. This feature proves that concurrent traveling of mobile agents is supported in our system model. Concurrency is an expected characteristic of our generic secure mobile agent system.

Proof: To prove this feature, we wrote the following query function in CPN ML:

fun concurrenttraveling(x, y: plat_tp_plat) : bool =
  (PredAllNodes (fn n=> cf(x, Mark.tokenpool'token_pool 1 n) > 0
        andalso
        cf(y, Mark.tokenpool'token_pool 1 n)>0)<>[]);

This function evaluates whether it is true that x and y, representing two different mobile agents respectively, can be in the token pool simultaneously. It evaluates to TRUE when x and y are replaced by different possible values of mobile agents in our system model. When a mobile agent travels, it is put into the token pool. So the TRUE result indicates that two mobile agents can travel concurrently.

8.5   Security

A wide range of security-related features of the sample system model can be investigated by using simulation-based analysis. Following are two of them.

Feature 6.

$\forall t, \forall j, \neg (Comm(MA_i, MAP_j) @ t) \{MA_i \infty MAP_k @ t, \ k \neq j\}$

Explanation: This formula states that a mobile agent cannot communicate directly with a platform other than its hosting platform. This feature shows that the communications between a mobile agent and other platforms must be forwarded and monitored by its hosting platform. It satisfies the requirement of the system and guarantees that a platform, which may be malicious, will not be able to interfere with the communications between a mobile agent and its current platform.

Proof: To prove this feature, we wrote the following function in CPN ML:

fun communicate_withothermap(x, y): bool =
(PredAllNodes (fn n=> cf(x, Mark.ma_strong1'P4 1 n)> 0
        andalso
    cf(y, Mark.ma_strong1'Pin 1 n) > 0) <> []);

This function evaluates whether it is true that a mobile agent locating on platform x can receive a message from another platform y. It evaluates to FALSE when x and y are different possible mobile agent platforms in our system. That means a mobile agent cannot receive a message from other platforms other than the one it resides on currently.

Feature 7.

$\forall t,\ Exec(MA_i, MAP_j)@t\ iff\ Supervised(MA_i, MAP_j)@t\quad \{MA_i\infty MAP_j\}$
Explanation: This formula states that a mobile agent can only be executed under its hosting platform's supervision. This feature protects a platform from unknown attacks from a malicious mobile agent and falls in the category of host security.
Proof: To prove this feature, the following function is written in CPN ML:

fun secureexecute_plat(x:status, y:packed_ma, z:simple_packma): bool
=

(PredAllNodes(fn n=>(cf(x, Mark.Reactive_action_ma1'P6 1 n)>0
orelse

        Cf(x, Mark.Autonomous_action_ma1'P7 1 n)>0)
        andalso
        ((Cf(y, Mark.Plat1_Execute_MA'Being_executed 1 n) <0
        andalso cf(z, Mark.plat1'Pmarec 1 n)>0)
        orelse
        (Cf(y, Mark.Plat2_Execute_MA'Being_executed 1 n) <0
        andalso cf(z, Mark.plat2'Pmarec 1 n)>0))<>[]);

This function evaluates whether it is true that when a mobile agent's actions (including reactive action and autonomous action) is performed while this mobile agent is NOT in the place "Being_executed" on its current mobile agent platform. It always evaluates to FALSE for different possible combinations of mobile agents and mobile agent platforms. As discussed in Section 4.2.1.3, place "Being_executed" is the secure execution place for a mobile agent because a mobile agent platform can reinforce security mechanisms like "sandbox" for that place. Therefore the FALSE result of this function guarantees that a mobile agent's execution will always be supervised and monitored by its current mobile agent platform. This feature protects a mobile agent platform from unknown attacks from a malicious mobile agent and falls in the category of host security.

Feature 8.

$\forall i, i', j, k, \exists t1, t2, (MA_i \infty MAP_j @ t1, MA_i \rightarrow MAP_k @(t1, t2), MA_{i'} \infty MAP_k @ t2) \Rightarrow MA_i = MA_{i'}$

Explanation: This formula states that a mobile agent will remain unchanged when it leaves one platform and arrives at another. This feature guarantees strong and secure mobility of mobile agents.

Proof : To prove this feature, the following function is written in CPN ML:

fun securetransfer((k1, (p1, pa1, (px1, mid1), (pk1, x))),
 (k2, (p2, pa2, (px2, mid2), (pk2, y)))): bool =
((PredAllNodes(fn n => (cf(EMa((k1, (p1, pa1, (px1, mid1), (pk1,x))))),
 Mark.Plat1'P2 1 n)>0)
 orelse cf(EMa((k1, (p1, pa1, (px1, mid1), (pk1, x))))),
 Mark.Plat2'P2 1 n)>0)<>[])
 andalso (PredAllNodes(fn m => (cf(EMa((k2, (p2, pa2, (px2, mid2),
(pk2, y))))),
 Mark.Plat1'P1 1 m)>0)
 orelse cf(EMa((k2, (p2, pa2, (px2, mid2), (pk2, y))))),
 Mark.Plat2'P1 1 m)>0)<>[])
andalso (px1=px2 andalso mid1=mid2 andalso pk1=pk2 andalso
x=y));

This function evaluates whether the mobile agent MA_i leaving platform MAP_j for another platform MAP_k is the same as the mobile agent $MA_{i'}$ arriving at platform MAP_k when this transfers terminates. It always evaluates to TRUE. That means our system supports secure and strong mobility of mobile agent.

The features discussed above are some examples of the analysis results based on simulation. The analysis that can be done is certainly not restricted to those mentioned above. As the framework we proposed is extendable and the mobile agent system model is generic, we can continue adding to the list of features by writing more functions in CPN ML to probe our model and analyze the results as well as the standard simulation report. We can also adopt the standard CPN analyze methods such as S-invariants and T-invariants.

Chapter 9

A Case Study in Electronic Commerce

9.1   Case Scenario

In this chapter, we use an electronic commerce application -- a flight ticket booking mobile agent as our case study. A flight ticket booking mobile agent has the following behaviors. It can migrate around an airline network according to its itinerary. It carries the information about expected ticket(s), such as round-trip/one way, date(s), approximate time, departure city, arrival city, and approximate price. After it arrives at a platform which sells flight tickets, it automatically inquires the platform's price information of the matched flights. If the platform provides tickets for such travel plan and the price meets the requirements of the agent, the mobile agent will book the ticket and return to its home platform afterwards. If not, the mobile agent will travel to other platforms. In this example, negotiation between the ticket booking mobile agent and the platform is not considered.

9.2   EEOS Model

The ticket booking mobile agent is illustrated in Figure 34, which is adapted from Figure 23. The transition **Inquire** is an autonomous action as this mobile agent, once it successfully arrives at a mobile agent platform and starts its execution, asks for the pricing information of a certain ticket from the airplane platform. The transitions **Compare**, **Accept** and **Reject** are all reactive actions, because firing them is triggered by certain messages received from the platform it travels to.

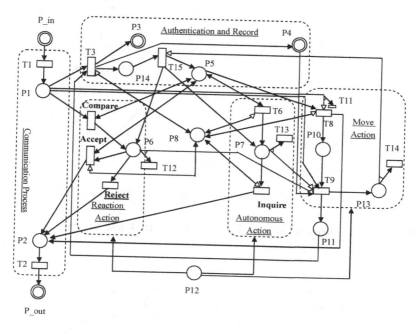

Figure 34 EEOS Model for the Simplified Flight Ticket Booking Mobile Agent

The high level EEOS model for mobile agent platform running on airplane sites remain the same. The **Execute** transition in Figure 19 is refined to include three different transitions **Report Price, Book Ticket** and **Dispatch** as shown in Figure 35.

The EEOS model of the trust server also remains the same, as the details of the mobile agent functionality and how it is to be executed is transparent to the trust server.

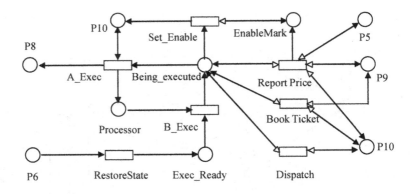

Figure 35 EEOS Model for the Flight Ticket Booking Mobile Agent Execution

9.3 Synchronous Firing Mechanism in the Case Study

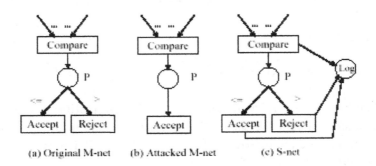

Figure 36 An Example of the Synchronous Firing Security Mechanism

In Figure 36 (a), the original mobile agent compares the price of the ticket offered by some other platform it travels to and the price it can afford when the provided ticket matches its requirements. If the price of some provided ticket is less than or equal to its own price, it will book that one and return to its home platform afterwards. If none of the provided tickets is cheaper than its own expected ticket, it will reject this platform and travel to other platforms. Figure 36 (c) is the S-net of (a). Each transition in (c) has interaction relation with its counterpart in (a). This means each transition in (c) will be decrypted by the firing of its counterpart transition in (a) and fired if it is enabled.

Suppose the flight ticket booking mobile agent has been attacked and part of the modified M-net is shown in Figure 36 (b). Certain malicious platform changes the structure of the ticket booking mobile agent and makes the agent book one of its tickets no matter how much higher its ticket price is over what the agent would afford. In this case, when the "Compare" transition produces a ">" token into place P, transition "Accept" will still be fired. But the S-net is not modified since we use encryption to prevent it from happening. Then when transition "Compare" fires in the modified M-net, the transition "Compare" will also fire in the S-net and produces the same token ">" to place P, as well as a record in its log place: $<t1, Compare, time1>$. Afterwards, the transition supposed to be fired should be transition "Reject", but since the counterpart transition "Reject" in M-net is removed and doesn't fire, the "Reject" transition in S-net still remains its encrypted version and cannot be fired. So the log of S-net only contains the record $<t1, Compare, time1>$. Although the M-net fires its "Accept" transition to book a ticket and decrypts the "Accept" transition in S-net, the "Accept" transition cannot fire in S-net since the token type in place P' is ">". Afterwards, this mobile agent travels back to its home platform. The home platform knows that the agent has booked a ticket on its behalf by checking the result the mobile agent returns. But when it checks the S-net state and Log, it finds that after "Compare", no "Accept" transition should be fired and the place P holding a token ">". Therefore, the home platform can detect that its mobile agent has been attacked by the platform on which a ticket is booked. It can go ahead and deny the service provided by the malicious platform and the security purpose of detection is achieved.

It should be mentioned here that the actions of this ticket booking mobile agent, such as "Compare", "Accept", and "Reject" are all considered as atomic actions. So they cannot be broken into sub-actions. The malicious platform can only remove some atomic actions, add some atomic actions, or repeat executing some atomic actions deliberately without changing the behavior of any atomic action. If some action can be broken into sub-actions, to use our synchronous firing security mechanism, we need to refine the action and consider those sub-actions when writing into the log places. In this circumstance, if the malicious platform adds some action or repeats executing some action, we can still possibly detect that tampering through the similar methods to the one we used above to detect removing action.

9.4   Design/CPN Model and Experiment Results

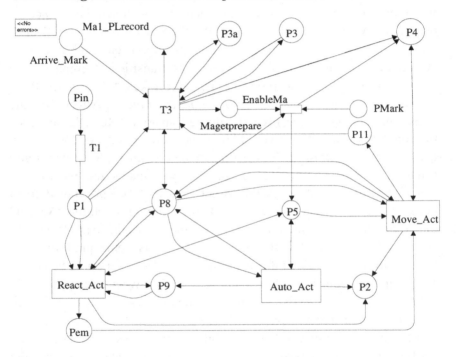

Figure 37 Top level Design/CPN model of the simplified flight ticket booking mobile agent

In the simplified flight ticket booking mobile agent system, there are two platforms and one mobile agent. Plat1 is the mobile agent's home platform. It creates the mobile agent which requests to move to the other platform Plat2 to acquire some new data, in this example, the price of a certain flight ticket. Figure 37, Figure 38 and Figure 39 show the top level Design/CPN models of the mobile agent, the mobile agent platform and the trust server in this simplified flight ticket booking mobile agent system.

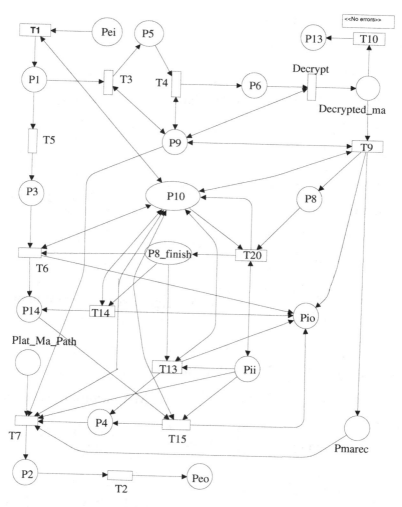

Figure 38 Top level Design/CPN model of the simplified flight ticket booking mobile agent platform

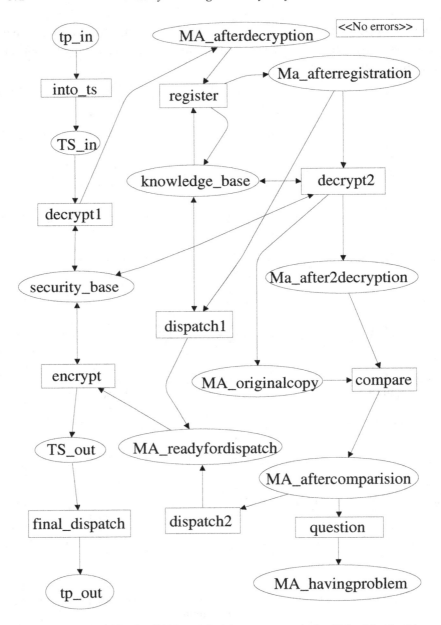

Figure 39 Top level Design/CPN model of the trust server in the flight ticket booking mobile agent system

As the original Design/CPN models are quite complex but the space here is limited, in order to present clear logic in these models, we do not include many detailed information in those models, such as CPN regions Color Set and Initial Marking for places, Code and Guard for transitions, Port place, Simulation Regions, and etc. In addition, many transitions in the top level, such as "React_Act" in Figure 34, are refined in the sub-pages, which are not shown here.

Our modeling and simulation are based on Design/CPN 4.0 on SunOS 5.8. The experiment results of this case study mobile agent system are consistent with the conclusions we get in chapter 8.

Chapter 10

A Case Study in E-auction System

10.1 Case Scenario

E-Auctions are negotiable trading activities carried out by trading agents whose interactions are governed by specific trading rules. They offer a number of advantages over conventional auction environment which constraint the sellers and buyers on a number of factors like geographical area, kind of products, time etc. They are cheaper to implement as the agents are programs and not humans. They are also based on conventional auction models like the English Auction, Dutch auction, Closed-bid auctions etc and are hence governed by well-known and well-understood trading rules. However there is certain trade-off's to be made. E-Auction systems have some very severe structural, security and reliability constraints. First, all the bidders and sellers need to have connectivity at all times. Second, authenticity, privacy, non-repudiation of users, integrity of data has to be maintained at all times. And third, there should be no favoring; the model should be fair and also reliable.

The structural requirements can at least partially be satisfied using Mobile agents, which perform all the bidding for the buyers by hoping between various merchant sites and which ensure that the user is free and off-line if necessary. Mobile agent technology offers a number of benefits like reduction of communication costs, better support for asynchronous tasks, support for dynamic protocols and intelligent data to name a few. Security constraints in the auction-model are then handled as security issues in mobile agent communication and information exchange.

10.1.1 *ABEAS - agent based e-auctioning system*

ABEAS is a close-bid mobile agent based e-auctioning system, in which the various functions typically carried out in any auctioning house are

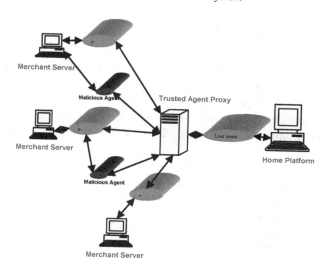

Figure 40 Block Diagram of the ABEAS System

carried out by the mobile agents, freeing the user's time and other resources and allowing them to carry on with their tasks. Figure 40 shows the block diagram of the ABEAS. Such an agent based system has a number of advantages:

(1) The user can perform other tasks when the agent does the actual bidding as a background operation.

(2) Mobile agents don't overlook details. They do precisely what they are told to do and in many cases intelligently do more.

(3) Mobile agents are rational agents, unlike their human counter parts.

The user creates an agent with his/her requirements: the price, the date by which the product has to be obtained, details about the product (color, dimensions and such) and sometimes even an itinerary of the servers. This mobile agent then goes to the various auctioning houses, compares the prices and if there is a matching product with a price lesser than the user's bid, places a bid and gives back the information to the user. The user looks at the proposals from various merchant sites and commits to the best match it finds.

10.1.1.1 *The agents in ABEAS*

There are two main mobile agents in an ABEAS, the E-Broker and the M-Agent. The E-Broker is the most important agent in the system. It collects the user requirements, goes to the various merchant sites, looks out and places bids and comes back to update the user and also performs the final committal function. This agent contains three kinds of information:

(1) Requirements for the Purchase: It contains the upper limit on the price the user is ready to pay, the product the user is looking to buy-the color, dimensions of the item and also the date by which the user wants the item.

(2) User Identification: There are multiple users in the ABEAS system placing multiple bids on various items, there needs to exist a mechanism for tracing the agents to the users who created them.

(3) Committal Function: This function is used by the agent to commit to a transaction on the user's behalf.

The M-Agent is an agent created by a malicious platform and is either a clone of an e-broker agent or is an agent to mislead created by a malicious merchant to falsely increase number of users and value of bids in the system. The clone agent pretends to be the original mobile agent and goes to visit the other platforms in the path history of the original mobile agent and comes back to the malicious platform with the values the other merchant platforms are offering for the same product. All this while the malicious platform holds on to the original mobile agent. When the clone gets back the malicious platform, fills out the path history of the clone agent and falsifies the prices offered by the other merchants in such a way that its offer is the best offer and sends the original agent back to its owner and kills the clone.

10.1.1.2 *The agent platform in ABEAS*

Mobile agents move around across various platforms and communicate with one another and also with other hosts. There are two basic approaches for modeling the agent platforms. The first approach is that the agent is sent to a 'trusted' designated platform to execute and it then communicates with the various merchant servers and collects information needed to commit to the purchases. The second approach is that the agent goes to each and every one of the merchant servers in turn, collects information and then finally goes back to the host or one of the merchant platforms to make a committal of the best bid.

Another agent platform model that is very practical and beneficial is one in which the requirements are communicated to a 'base' platform, which in turn creates agents that can move between the merchant servers in any one of the above stated approaches.

For such a model to be successful the assumption is that the 'base' platform is one that is trusted completely. In our model, the 'base' platform is nothing but the Trusted Agent Proxy and we use the approach in which the mobile agent goes to and from the Trusted Agent Proxy to the various merchant platforms and finally goes back to the owner from the trusted agent proxy.

10.1.1.3 *Security issues in the ABEAS*

The main security issues in the ABEAS include the following. Firstly, the committal function which carries out the actual "buy" operation needs to be designed with care. What kind of financial means is used to pay for the transaction has to be decided by credit or by E-tokens and such. Another issue with the committal function is that some users may prefer to remain anonymous. In this case, user identify has to be maintained and at the same time authentication of the user also has to be done. Secondly, the malicious platform attacks like Path history changes, mobile agent pricing information changes, clone agent creation, withholding the e-broker agent, non-repudiation and mislead agent creation needs to be addressed. Thirdly, malicious agent attacks to platforms like denial of service (DoS) need to be addressed. These problems can be solved by adding certain features to the 'Base' Platform. Such a fine-tuned platform is called the Trusted Agent Proxy in the ABEAS system.

10.1.2 *Modeling requirements of ABEAS*

In order to completely understand any system, the first step would be to model the system, using standard modeling tools; the model of a system will help us understand the actual working of the system and help to identify the problem areas. While selecting a modeling tool for the ABEAS system, the following things have to be kept in mind. First, the mobile agent - platform communication will have to be modeled. Second, the mobile agent - mobile agent communication will have to be modeled. And third, the Modeling tool will have to have a provision for incorporating a security mechanism and should facilitate the modeling of such a mechanism.

10.2   EEOS Model

In this section, we apply the generic model of the mobile agent system to the ABEAS auctioning environment. Both the agent system and the Trusted Server have to be are modified to suit the auctioning application.

10.2.1 *The e-broker agent*

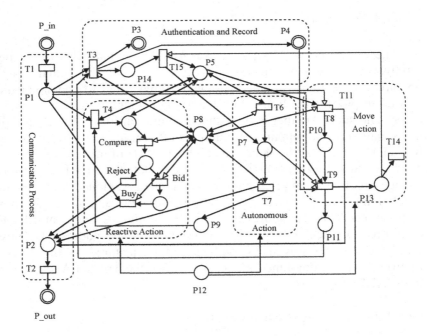

Figure 41 The EEOS Model of the E-Broker Agent

Figure 41 shows the EEOS model of the E-Broker agent. The meanings of some special places are as follows. P6 is to store the synchronization token for the co-ordination between the three kinds of actions and to enable/disable the mobile agent. P9 is to store token placed by the Inquire action (autonomous action) to indicate that the next action is the Reactive action. P18 is a database containing the security and the user ratings, which is actually in the proxy server but which is updated by both the mobile agent and the mobile agent platform. Compares, Reject, Buy and Bid are transitions that as their names indicate are used for the auction operations.

The e-broker compares the price it is ready to pay(from place P6) and the price that is provided by the mobile agent platform(from P8) and if the value is lesser or equal to the amount it is ready to pay it goes ahead and bids (Bid Transition)for the item and sends the information to the proxy server. It also updates a user rating database in the trusted proxy, in which a good rating is given to the platform (merchant) if a bid is placed and a bad rating is given if the bid is rejected. The trusted proxy collects the information from all the platforms and then finally sends the information to the user platform along with the rating database. The user can now take his decision on whether he wants to buy from maybe a good trusted platform with a higher price than a "bad" platform with a lesser platform, using the database. If the user commits to a buy then the mobile agent goes back and completes the transaction and adds to the rating of the site for the particular user.

10.2.2 *The modified trust server*

The Trust server decrypts the incoming mobile agent, checks with the trust model to determine whether a second level of encryption is needed and then finishes the registration with its registration table, establishes a proxy key for the source, and adds a session key for the particular mobile agent platform, starts a timer and sends the mobile agent to the destination platform.

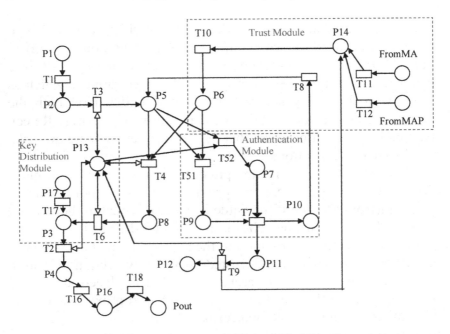

Figure 42 The EEOS Model of the Modified Trust Server

Figure 42 illustrates the EEOS model of the modified Trust Server. The meanings of some special places/transitions are as follows. Pin, Pout are the incoming and outgoing places of the TAP. P17 holds the session key; P13 is the key distribution center holding the proxy, private and public key information. P14 is the trust rating database that is updated by both MA and MAP. T16 sets the timer. The rest of the transition and places are the same as in the generic case.

Chapter 11

Conclusion

In this book, we discussed the security problem in a mobile agent system. The security problem has become a bottleneck for the development of mobile agent technology. We summarized the requirements for a secure mobile agent system and gave a comprehensive survey of existing methods to solve this problem. We proposed a new formal method - Extended Elementary Object System (EEOS) to model a generic secure mobile agent system. Based on the modeling mechanism, we proposed a hierarchical model for a generic secure mobile agent system, which includes the mobile agent platform level, the mobile agent level and the security mechanism level. Several security mechanisms are proposed for securely transferring a mobile agent, mutual authentication between a mobile agent and a mobile agent platform, authorization of a mobile agent platform to mobile agents, and secure execution of a mobile agent on a mobile agent platform. How to translate an EEOS model into a colored Petri Net model and how to simulate it in Design/CPN are among our contributions. We also study two cases in electronic commerce and in E-auction.

Bibliography

[1]. Anderson, D., Lunt, Javitz, T. F., Tamaru, H., A. and Valdes, A.,
"Detecting Unusual Program Behavior Ising the Statistical Component
of the Next-Generation Intrusion Detection Expert System (NIDES),"
SRI International Computer Science Laboratory Technical Report SRI-
CSL-95-07, May 1995.

[2]. "FAQ about Jumping Beans," Jumping Beans Inc., February 2004,
http://www.JumpingBeans.com/.

[3]. Accorsi, R., Basin, D., and Vigano, L., "Modal Specifications of Trace-
Based Security Properties," *Proceedings of the Second International
Workshop on Security of Mobile Multiagent Systems,* Bologna, Italy,
July 2002.

[4]. Asperti, A., and Busi, N., "Mobile Petri Nets," *Technical Report
UBLCS96-10,* University of Bologna, May 1996.

[5]. Badouel, E., and Oliver, J., "Reconfigurable Nets, A Class of high Level
Petri Nets Supporting Dynamic Changes within Workflow Systems,"
INRIA Research Report, PI-1163, 1998.

[6]. Baek, J., "A Design of A Protocol For Detecting A Mobile Agent Clone
And Its Correctness Proof Using Coloured Petri Nets," *Technical Report
TR-DIC-CSL-1998-002, K-JIST,* 1998.

[7]. Baldassari, M., Bruno, G., "PROTOB: an Object Oriented Methodology
for Developing Discrete Event Dynamic Systems," *Computer
Languages,* vol. 16, no. 1, pp. 39 – 63, 1991.

[8]. Bastide, R., "Approaches in Unifying Petri Nets and the Object Oriented
Approach," *Proceedings of 16th International Conference on
Application and Theory of Petri nets, 1st Workshop on Object-Oriented
Programming and Models of Concurrency,* June 1995.

[9]. Bastide, R., and Palanque, P., "Cooperative Objects: a Concurrent Petri
net based Object-Oriented Language," *Proceedings of IEEE Conf.
System Man and Cybernetics,* October 1993.

[10]. Bates, J., "The State of the Art in Distributed and Dependable
Computing," *Technical Report ESPRIT Cabernet Sponsored Report,*
University of Cambridge, UK, October 1998.

183

[11]. Baumann, J., "Mobile Agents: Control Algorithms," *Lecture Notes in Computer Science*, Vol. 1658, 2000.

[12]. Baumann, J., Hohl, F., Roghermel, L., and Straβer, M., "Mole – Concepts of a Mobile Agent System," *World Wide Web Journal, special issue on Distributed World Wide Web Processing: Applications and Techniques of Web Agents*, 1998. 1.1.1.

[13]. Biberstein, O., Buchs, D., and Guelfi, N., "A Specification Language for Distributed Systems Engineering," *Technical Report 96/167*, Swiss Federal Institute of Technology, Lausanne, 1996.

[14]. Bishop, M., "Computer Security – Art and Science," Addison-Wesley, ISBN 0-201-44099-7, 2002.

[15]. V. Bontchev, "Possible Virus Attacks against Integrity Programs and How to Prevent Them," http://vx.netlux.org/lib/static/vdat/epposatt.htm.

[16]. Brewington, R., Gray, R., and Moizumi, K., "Mobile Agents in Distributed Information Retrieval," *Intelligent Information Agents*, edited by Mathias Klusch, Springer Verlag, Chapter 15, pp. 355-395, 1999.

[17]. Bryce, C., "A Security Framework for A Mobile Agent System," *Proceedings of the 2nd International Workshop on Security in Mobile Multiagent Systems (SEMAS 2002)*, Bologna, Italy , July , 2002.

[18]. Burkhard, H.-D., "Software-Architectures for Agents and Mobile Robots," *Proceedings of the Second International Workshop on Modelling of Objects, Components, and Agents (MOCA'02)*, Aarhus, Denmark, August 26-27, pp.1- 18 2002.

[19]. Cardelli, L., "Abstractions for Mobile Computation," *Secure Internet Programming, Security Issues for Mobile and Distributed Objects*, Lecture Notes in Computer Science 1603, Springer, pp. 51- 94, 1999.

[20]. Cardelli, L., and Gordon, A. D., "Mobile Ambients," *Proceedings of First International Conference of Foundations of Software Science and Computation Structure:*, FOSSACS '98.

[21]. Cardelli, L., and Gordon, A.D., "Types for the Ambient Calculus," *Proceedings of 26th Annual ACM Symposium on Principles of Programming Languages*, pp. 79 – 92, 1999.

[22]. Cao, J., Feng, X., Lu, J., and Das, S. K., "Design of Adaptive and Reliable Mobile Agent Communication Protocols," *Proceedings of the 22nd International Conference on Distributed Computing Systems (ICDCS'02)*, Vienna, Austria, pp. 471-476, July 2-5, 2002.

[23]. CERT Coordination Center Denial of Service, http://www.cert.org/tech_tips/denial_of_service.html.

[24]. Ceska, M., and Janousek V, "A Formal Model for Object Oriented Petri Nets Modeling," *Advances in Systems Science and Applications*, An Official Journal of the International Institute for General Systems Studies, Special Issue, 1997.

[25]. Chan, A.H. W., Wong, L.M., Wong, T.Y., and Lyu, M.R., "Securing Mobile Agents for Electronic Commerce: An Experiment," *Proceedings of Fifteenth Annual Working Conference on Information Security*, Beijing, China, pp. 471-480, August 22-24, 2000.

[26]. Chess, D., Harrison, C., and Kershenbaum, A., "Mobile Agents: Are They a Good Idea?," *IBM Research report*, J. Watson Research Center, March 1995.

[27]. Chess, D., Grosof, B., and Harrison, C., "Itinerant Agents for Mobile Computing," *IEEE Personal Communications*, pp. 34 – 49, October 1995.

[28]. Chess, D., "Security Issues in Mobile Code Systems," *Mobile Agents and Security*, Giovanni Vigna (Ed.), Springer-Verlag, pp. 1- 14, 1998.

[29]. Christensen, S., "Modelling with Coloured Petri Nets," *Proceedings of the Second International Workshop on Modelling of Objects, Components, and Agents (MOCA'02), Aarhus, Denmark, August 26-27, 2002.*

[30]. Cost, R. S., Chen, Y., Finin, T., Labrou, Y., and Peng Y., "Modeling Agent Conversations with Colored Petri Nets," *Working Notes of the Workshop on Specifying and Implementing Conversation Policies, Autonomous Agents '99*, Seattle, Washington, May 1999.

[31]. Cremonini, M., Omicini, A., andZambonelli, F., "Modeling Network Topology and Mobile Agent Interaction: An Integrated Framework," *Proceedings of the 1999 ACM symposium on Applied computing (SAC'99)*, pp. 410 – 412, 1999.

[32]. Dillenseger B., "MobiliTools: A Toolbox for Agent Mobility and Interoperability Based on PMG Standards," *Proceedings of 2nd International Symposium on Agent Systems and Applications, 4th International Symposium on Mobile Agents*, Zürich, September, 2000.

[33]. Elliot, M., Billington, J., and Kristensen L. M., "Using Design/CPN to Design a Visualization Extension for Design/CPN," *Proceedings of the Fourth International Workshop on Practical Use of Colored Petri Nets and the CPN Tools, Aarhus, Denmark*, pp. 21-38, August 28-30, 2002.

[34]. Esser, R., "An Object Oriented Petri net Language for Embedded System Design," *Proceedings of the 8th International Workshop on Software Technology and Engineering Practice incorporating Computer Aided Software Engineering*, pp. 216-223, London 1997.

[35]. Farmer, W. M., Guttmann, J D., and Swarup V., "Security for Mobile Agents: Authentication and State Appraisal," *Proceedings of the Fourth European Symposium on Research in Computer Security*, pp. 118-130, 1996.

[36]. Farmer, W. M., Guttmann, J D., and Swarup V., "Security for Mobile Agents: Issues and Requirements," *Proceedings of the 19th National Information Systems Security Conference*, vol. 2, pp. 591-597, 1996.

[37]. Feigenbaum, J., and Lee, P., "Trust Management and Proof-Carrying Code in Secure Mobile-Code Applications," DARPA *Workshop on Foundations for Secure Mobile Code in Monterey*, March 26-28, 1997.

[38]. Fernandes, J. M., and Belo, O., "Modeling Multi-Agent Systems Activities Through Colored Petri Nets," *Proceedings of 16th IASTED International Conference on Applied Informatics*, Germany, Fevereiro 1998.

[39]. Fernandez, E. B., "An Overview of Internet Security," *Proceedings of the World's Internet & Electronic Cities Conference (WIECC 2001)*, Kish Island, Iran, May 1-3, 2001.

[40]. Ferreira, L., Zuquete, A., Ferreira, P., "SEFS: Security Module for Extensible File System Architectures," *Proceedings of European Conference on Information Security Solutions (ISSE)*, Barcelona, September 2000.

[41]. Firewall Software White Paper, http://www.firewall-software.com/firewall_faws/types_of_firewall.html

[42]. Forman, G. H., "The Challenges of Mobile Computing," *IEEE Computer*, pp. 38 - 47, 1994.

[43]. Fournet, C., and Gonthier, G., "A Calculus of Mobile Agents," *Proceedings of the 7th International Conference on Concurrency Theory (CONCUR '96)*, LNCS 1119, pp. 406 - 421, 1996.

[44]. Fuggetta, A., Picco, G. P., and Vigna, G., "Understanding Code Mobility," *IEEE Transactions on Software Engineering*, Vol. 24, No. 5, pp 342- 361, May 1998.

[45]. Giovanni, D., "HOOD Nets," *Advances in Petri Nets,* LNCS 524, Springer, Berlin, pp. 140 – 160, 1991.

[46]. Gong, L., "Survivable Mobile code is Hard to Build," *Proceedings of DARPA Workshop on Foundations for Secure Mobile Code Workshop*, pp. 26 – 28, March 1997.

[47]. Gordon, A. D., "Nominal Calculi for Security and Mobility," *Proceedings of DARPA Workshop on Foundations for Secure Mobile Code*, pp. 10 - 14, 1997.

[48]. Gordon, A.D., "Notes on Nominal Calculi for Security and Mobility," *Foundations of Security Analysis and Design, LNCS 2171*, pp. 262 – 330, 2002.

[49]. Gray, R., "Mobile Agents for Mobile Computing," *Technical Report PCS-TR96-285*, Dartmouth College, Computer Science, Hanover, NH, May 1996.

[50]. Gray, R. S., "Agent Tcl: A Flexible and Secure Mobile Agent System," *Proceedings of Fourth Annual Usenix Tcl/Tk Workshop*, pp. 9- 23, 1996.

[51]. Gray, R. S., Kotz, D., Cybenko, G. and Rus, D., "D'Agents: Security in a Multiple-Language, Mobile-Agent System," *Mobile Agents and Security*, pp. 154 -187, 1998.

[52]. Gray, R., Kotz, D., Cybenko, G., Rus, D., "Mobile Agents: Motivations and State-of-the-art Systems," *Technical Report TR2000-365*, Dept. of Computer Science, Dartmouth College.

[53]. Gray, R., "Mobile Agents for Mobile Computing," *Technical Report PCS-TR96-285*, Department of Computer Science, Dartmouth College.

[54]. Guelfi, N., Biberstein, O., and Buchs, D, Canver, E., Gaudel, M-C., Henke, and F., Schwier, D., "Comparison of Object Oriented Formal Methods," *Technical Report of the Esprit Long Term Research Project 20072 ``Design For Validation''*, University of Newcastle Upon Tyne, Department of Computing Science, 1997.

[55]. Hagimont, D., and Ismail, L., "A Protection Scheme for Mobile Agents on Java," *Proceedings of MobiCom: 3rd ACM/IEEE International Conference on Mobile Computing and Networking*, pp. 215 – 222, 1997.

[56]. Hiraishi, K., "A Petri-Net-Based Model for the Mathematical Analysis of Multi-Agent Systems," *IEICE Transactions on Fundamentals*, vol. E84 A, no.11, pp. 2829 – 1837, November 2001.

[57]. Hohl, F., "An Approach to Solve the Problem of Malicious Hosts in Mobile Agent Systems," *Proceedings of 4th ECOOP Workshop on Mobility: Secure Internet Mobile Computations*, 1998.

[58]. Hohl, F., "A Model of Attacks of Malicious Hosts Against Mobile Agents," *Proceedings of the ECOOP Workshop on Distributed Object Security and 4th Workshop on Mobile Object Systems: Secure Internet Mobile Computations*, pp. 105 - 120, INRIA, France, 1998.

[59]. Hohl, F., "Time Limited Blackbox Security: Protecting Mobile Agents from Malicious Hosts," *Mobile Agents and Security*, Lecture Notes in Computer Science, vol. 1419, pp. 92-113, 1998.

[60]. Holvoet, T., "Agents and Petri Nets," *Petri Net Newsletter*, no. 49, pp. 3-8, October 1995.

[61]. Hutter, D., and Fischer, L., "Discussion: Towards a Methodology for the Design of Secure Mobile Multiagent Systems," *Proceedings of First International Workshop on Security of Mobile Multiagent Systems*, May 2001.

[62]. Ismail, L., and Hagimont, D., "A Performance Evaluation of the Mobile Agent Paradigm," *ACM SIGPLAN Notices*, 34(10), pp. 306-313, October 1999.

[63]. Jansen, W. A., "Countermeasures for Mobile Agent Security," *Computer Communications, Special Issue on Advanced Security Techniques for Network Protection*, Elsevier Science BV, November 2000.

[64]. Jansen, W. A., Karygiannis, T., "Mobile Agents and Security," *National Institute of Standards and Technology, Special Publication 800-19*, August 1999.

[65].   Jansen, W. A., "A Privilege Management Scheme for Mobile Agent Systems," *Autonomous Agents conference*, Montreal, Canada, May 2001,.

[66].   Jensen, K., "Coloured Petri Nets: A High Level Language for System Design and Analysis," *Advances in Petri Nets*, Lecture Notes in Computer Science 4831, 990.

[67].   Johansen, D., Renessen, R., and Schneider, F., "An Introduction to the TACOMA Distributed System," *Technical Report 95-23*, Department of Computer Science, University of Tromsø, June 1995.

[68].   Johansen, D., Schneider, F. and Renessen, R., "What TACOMA taught us," *Mobility, Mobile Agents and Process Migration – An Edited Collection*, Addison Wesley, 1998.

[69].   Kappel, G., and Schrefl, M., "Using An Object-Oriented Diagram Technique for the Design of Information Systems," *Dynamic Modelling of Information Systems*, Amsterdam, New York, 1991.

[70].   Karjoth, G., Lange, D. B., and Oshima, M., "A Security Model for Aglets," *Mobile Agents and Security*, Giovanni Vigna (Ed.), Springer-Verlag, pp. 188 – 205, 1998.

[71].   Karnik, N., Tripathi, A., "Agent Server Architecture for the Ajanta Mobile-Agent System," *Proceedings of the 1998 International Conference on Parallel and Distributed Processing Techniques and Applications (PDPTA'98)*, pp. 66 – 73, July 1998.

[72].   Keller, R. K., Shen, X., and Bochmann, G., "A Simple, yet Expressive and Flexible Formalism for Business Modelling," *Proceedings of the Workshop on Computer-Supported Cooperative Work, Petri Nets and Related Formalisms*, pp. 51-55, Zaragoza, Spain, June 1994.

[73].   Kim, S.-H., and Robertazzi, T. G, "Mobile Agent Modeling," *Technical Report No. 786*, University at Stony Brook, College of Engineering and Applied Science, Nov. 30, 2000.

[74].   Knabe, F., "An Overview of Mobile Agent Programming," *Proceedings of the Fifth LOMAPS workshop on Analysis and Verification of Multiple - Agent Languages*, no. 1192 in LNCS. Springer-Verlag, 1996.

[75].   Knorr, K., and Röhrig, S., "Security of Electronic Business Applications: Structure and Quantification," *Proceedings of First International Conference on Electronic Commerce and Web Technologies*, pp. 25 – 37, 2000.

[76].   Ko, C., Ruschitzka, M., and Levitt, K., "Execution Monitoring of Security-Critical Programs in Distributed System: A Specification-Based Approach," *Proceedings of the 1997 IEEE Symposium on Security and Privacy*, pp. 175-187, May 1997.

[77].   Köhler, M., Moldt, D., and Rölke, H., "Modelling the Structure and Behavior of Petri Net Agents," *Proceedings of 22nd International*

Conference on Application and Theory of Petri Nets (ICATPN 2001), pp. 224 – 241, 2001.

[78]. Köhler, M., and Rölke, H., "Modelling Mobility and Mobile Agents Using Nets Within Nets," *Proceedings of the Second International Workshop on Modelling of Objects, Components, and Agents (MOCA'02)*, pp. 141 – 157, Aarhus, Denmark, August 26-27, 2002.

[79]. Kotzanikolaou, P., Burmester, M., and Chrissikopoulos, V., "Secure Transactions with Mobile Agents in Hostile Environments," *ACISP 2000*, LNCS 1841, pp. 289 – 297, 2000.

[80]. Kraus, S., Wilkenfeld, J., and Zlotkin, G., "Multiagent Negotiation Under Time Constraints," *Artificial Intelligence Journal 75(2)*, pp. 297-345, 1995.

[81]. Kuhn, T. A. and Oheimb, D., "Interacting State Machines for Mobility Formal Methods," *Proceedings of the International Symposium of Formal Methods,* Lecture Notes in Computer Science, vol. 2805, pp 698-718, September 8-14, 2003.

[82]. Kumar, S., and Spafford, E., "A Pattern Matching Model for Misuse Intrusion Detection," *Proceedings of the 17th National Computer Security Conference*, pp. 11 – 21, October 1994.

[83]. Lakos, C., "From Coloured Petri Nets to Object Petri Nets," *Proceeding of the 16th International Conference on Application and Theory of Petri Nets*, pp. 278 – 297, Turin, June 1995.

[84]. Lakos, C., "The Object Orientation of Object Petri Nets," *Proceedings of the First International Workshop on ``Object Oriented Programming and Models of Concurrency'' within the 16th International Conference on Application and Theory of Petri Nets*, pp. 1 – 14, June 1995.

[85]. Lakos, C., "Object Oriented Modelling with Object Petri Nets," *Concurrent Object-Oriented Programming and Petri Nets*, G. Agha, F.D. Cindio, and G. Rozenberg (eds.), Lecture Notes in Computer Science 2001, Springer-Verlag 2001.

[86]. Lee, P., Necula, G., "Research on Proof-Carrying Code for Mobile-Code Security," *Proceedings of DARPA Workshop on Foundations for Secure Mobile Code* , March 1997.

[87]. Li, X., Xu, X. and Rosano, F. L., "Modeling manufacturing systems using object-oriented colored Petri nets," *International Journal of Intelligent Control Systems*, vol. 3, no. 3, pp. 359-375, 1999.

[88]. Liberman, B., Griffel, F., Merz, M., and Lamersdorf, W., "Java_based Mobile Agents – How to Migrate, Persist, and Interact on Electronic Service Markets," *Proceedings of Mobile Agents 97 Workshop*, Berlin, Springer LNCS #1219 1997.

[89]. Liew, C.-C., Ng, W.-K., Lim, E.-P., Tan, B.-S., and Ong, K.-L., "Non-Repudiation in An Agent-Based Electronic Commerce System,"

Proceedings of the International Workshop on Electronic Commerce and Security, Florence, Italy, August 30 - September 3, 1999.

[90]. Ling, S., and Schmidt, H. W., "A Notion of Safeness in Time for Petri Nets," *Proceedings of International Software Engineering Conference (IASTED-SE 97)*, San Francisco, pp. 344-350, 1997.

[91]. Lingnau, A., and Drobnic, O., "An Infrastructure for Mobile Agents: Requirements and Architecture," *Proceedings of 13th DIS Workshop*, Orlando, Florida, September 1995.

[92]. Loureiro S., Molva, R., and Pannetrat A., "Secure Data Collection with Updates," *Electronic Commerce Research*, vol. 1, no. 1-2, pp. 119-131, 2001.

[93]. Lwe, M., Wikarski, D., and Han, Y., "Higher-Order Object Nets and their Application to Workflow Modeling," *Research Report 95-34*, FB Informatik, Technical University Berlin, 1995.

[94]. Ma, L., and Tsai, J. J.P., "Formal Verification Techniques for Communication Security Protocols," *Handbook of Software Engineering and Knowledge Engineering*, 2001.

[95]. Ma, L., Tsai, J. J.P., and Murata, T., "Modeling a Secure Mobile Agent System with Petri nets Scheme," *Proceedings of 12th Information Security Conference*, pp. 399-406, Taiwan, May 16-17, 2002.

[96]. Ma, L., Tsai, J. J.P., Deng, Y., and Murata, T., "Extended Elementary Object System Model for Mobile Agent Security," *Proceedings of 2003 World Congress on Integrated Design and Process Technology*, pp. 169 – 178, Dec 3-6, 2003.

[97]. Ma, L., and Tsai, J.J.P., "A Secure Mobile Agent System Model Based on Extended Elementary Object Net," *Proceedings of 25th IEEE Int'l Computer Software and Applications Conference,* pp. 218-223, Sept. 2004.

[98]. Ma, L., and Tsai, J. J.P., "Attacks and Countermeasures in Software System Security," *Handbook of Software Engineering and Knowledge Engineering*, Vol. III, 2005.

[99]. Marsan, M. A., Balbo, G., and Conte, G., "A Class of Generalized Stochastic Petri Nets for the Performance Evaluztion of Multiprocessor Systems," *ACM transactions on Computer Science*, vol. 2, no. 2, pp. 93 - 122, May 1984.

[100]. Meadows, C., "Detecting Attacks on Mobile Agents," *Proceedings of 1997 Foundations for Secure Mobile Code Workshop*, pp. 64 - 65, Monterey, CA, March 1997.

[101]. Meseguer, J., and Talcott, C., "Rewriting Logic and Secure Mobility," *Proceedings of DARPA Workshop on Foundations for Secure Mobile Code Workshop*, pp. 26 – 28, March 1997.

[102]. Mitrović, N., and Arribalzaga, U. A., "Mobile Agent Security Using Proxy-Agents and Trusted Domains," *Proceedings of Second International Workshop on Security of Mobile Multiagent Systems*, 2002.

[103]. Moore, J. T., "Mobile code Security Techniques," *Technical Report MIS-CIS-98-28*, Department of Computer and Information Science, University of Pennsylvania, May 1998.

[104]. Mudumbai, S., Essiari, A., and Johnston, W., "Anchor Toolkit (A Secure Mobile Agent System)," *Proceedings of Mobile Agents '99 Conference*, October 1999.

[105]. Muhugusa, M., "Implementing Distributed Services with Mobile Code: the Case of the Messenger Environment," *Proceedings of the IASTED International Conference on Parallel and Distributed Systems (Euro-PDS'98)*, Austria, July 1998.

[106]. Murata, T., "Petri Nets: Properties, Analysis, and Applications," *Proceedings of the IEEE*, pp. 541 – 580, April 1989.

[107]. Necula, G. C., and Lee, P., "Safe Kernel Extensions without Run-Time Checking," *Proceedings of Second Symposium on Operating Systems Design and Implementation (OSDI '96)*, Seattle, Washington, October 28-31, 1996.

[108]. Necula, G. C., "Proof-Carrying Code," *Proceedings of the 24th Annual ACM SIGPLAN-SIGACT Symposium on Principles of Programming Languages (POPL'97)*, Paris, Fance, January 15-17, 1997.

[109]. Necula, G. C., and Lee, P., "Safe, Untrusted Agents Using Proof-Carrying Code," *Mobile Agents and Security*, pp. 61 – 91, Springer-Verlag (1998).

[110]. Neuendorf, K.-P., and Hannebauer, M., "Formal Modeling of Multi-Agent Interaction in Distributed Scheduling," *Proceedings of the 16th IMACS World Congress on Scientific Computation, Applied Mathematics and Simulation (IMACS-2000)*. Lausanne, Switzerland, 2000.

[111]. Newman, A., Shatz, S. M., and Xie, X., "An Approach to Object System Modeling by State-Based Object Petri Nets," *International Journal of Circuits, Systems, and Computers*, vol. 8, no. 1, pp. 1 – 20, Feb. 1998.

[112]. Nguyen, A, Stewart, I. and Yang, X., "A Mobile Agent Model: Applications for E-Commerce," *Proceedings of Seventh Australian World Wide Web Conference*, pp. 21 – 25, April 2001.

[113]. Noordende, G., Trazier, F. M.T., and Tanenbaum, A. S., "A Security Framework for a Mobile Agent System," *Proceedings of 6th European Symposium on Research in Computer Security (ESORICS 2000)*, pp. 273 – 290, 2000.

[114]. Object Petri Net Research at the University of Adelaide, http://www.cs.adelaide.edu.au/ charles/OPN.html.

[115]. "ObjectSpace Voyager Core Package Technical Overview," ObjectSpace, Inc., December 1997.

[116]. Omicini, A., and Zambonelli, F., "TuCSoN: a Coordination Model for Mobile Information Agents," *Proceedings of 1st Workshop on Innovative Internet Information Systems '98 (IIIS '98)*, June 1998.

[117]. Ordille, J. J., "When Agents Roam, Who Can You Trust?" *Proceedings of 1st Annual Conf. Emerging Technologies and Applications in Communications*, 1996.

[118]. Orso, A., Vigna, G. and Harrold, M. J., "MASSA: Mobile Agents Security through Static/Dynamic Analysis," *Proceedings of the ICSE Workshop on Software Engineering and Mobility,* May 2001.

[119]. Ousterbout, J. K., Levy, J. Y., and Welch, B. B., "The Safe-Tcl Security Model," *Technical Report TR-97-60*, Sun Microsystem Laboratories, 1997.

[120]. Park, S., Kim, J. and Lee, S., "Agent-Oriented Software Modeling with UML Approach," *IEICE Transactions on Information & System*, vol.E83-D, no.8, pp. 1631 – 1641, August 2000.

[121]. Patra, M. R., amd Moore, R., "A Formal Model of an Agent-Mediated Electronic Market," *Proceedings of The DIISM 2000 conference*, November 15 - 17 2000.

[122]. Peine, H., and Stolpmann, T., "The Architecture for the Ara Platform for Mobile Agents," *Proceedings of the First International Workshop on Mobile Agents (MA'97)*, vol. 1219 of Lecture Notes in Computer Science pp. 50 – 61, 1997.

[123]. Picco, G. P., Roman, G. C., and Mccann, P. J., "Reasoning About Code Mobility in Mobile UNITY", *ACM Transactions on Software Engineering and Methodology (TOSEM)*, vol. 10, no. 3, pp. 338-395, July 2001.

[124]. Puliafito, A. and Tomarchio, O., "Security Mechanisms for the MAP Agent System," *Proceedings of the 8th Euromicro Workshop on Parallel and Distributed Processing*, pp. 84-91, January 19-21, 2000.

[125]. Roman, G. C., and Payton, J., "Mobile UNITY Schemas for Agent Coordination," *Proceedings of the 10th International Workshop on Abstract State Machines, LNCS 2589*, Springer, pp. 126-150, March 2003.

[126]. Roth, V., "Secure Recording of Itineraries through Co-operating Agents," *Proceedings of ECOOP'98 Workshops*, Lecture Notes in Computer Science 1543, pp. 297-298, July 20-24, 1998.

[127]. Roth, V., "On the Robustness of Some Cryptographic Protocols for Mobile Agent Protection," *Proceedings of the 5th International Conference MA 2001*, LNCS 2240, pp. 1- 14, Atlanta, GA, December 2 - 4 , 2001.

[128]. Rothermel, K., Hohl, F., and Radouniklis, N., "Mobile Agent Systems: What is Missing?," *Proceedings of International Working Conference on Distributed Applications and Interoperable Systems (DAIS'97)*, pp. 111-124, Cottbus, Germany, September 30, 1997.

[129]. Saldhana, J. A., and Shatz, S. M., "UML Diagrams to Object Petri Net Models: An Approach for Modeling and Analysis," *Proceedings of the Int. Conference on Software Engineering and Knowledge Engineering (SEKE)*, pp. 103 – 110, Chicago, July 2000.

[130]. Sander, T., and Tschudin, C. F., "On the Cryptographic Protection of Mobile Code," *Proceedings of Workshop on Mobile Agents and Security*, October 1997.

[131]. Sander, T., and Tschudin, C. F., "Towards Mobile Cryptography," *Proceedings of IEEE Symposium on Security and Privacy*, pp. 215 - 224, May 1998.

[132]. Sander, T., and Tschudin, C. F., "Protecting Mobile Agents Against Malicious Hosts," *Mobile Agents and Security*, Lecture Notes in Computer Science 1419, pp. 44 – 60, 1998.

[133]. Sander, T., and Tschudin, C. F., "On Software Protection via Function Hiding," *Proceedings of the 2nd Workshop on Information Hiding*, LNCS vol. 1525, pp.111 – 123, April 1998.

[134]. Sandhu, R. S., Samarati, P., "Authentication, Access Control, and Intrusion Detection," *The Computer Science and Engineering Handbook*, CRC Press, Boca Raton, FL, 1997.

[135]. Satoh, I., "Hierarchically Structured Mobile Agents and Their Migration," *Proceedings of Workshop on Mobile Object Systems (MOS'99)*, 1999.

[136]. Schneck, P. A., and Schwan, K., "Dynamic Allocation of Security Resources to Client-Server Applications," *Proceedings of IEEE Workshop on Dependable and Real-Time E-Commerce Systems*, May 1998.

[137]. Serugendo, G. D. M., Muhugusa, M., and Tschudin, C. F., "A Survey of Theories for Mobile Agents," *World Wide Web Journal, special issue on Distributed World Wide Web Processing: Applications and Techniques of Web Agents*, vol.1, no.3, pp. 139 - 153, 1998.

[138]. Shehory, O., Sycara, K., Chalasani, P., and Jha, S., "Agent Cloning: an Approach to Agent Mobility and Resource Allocation," *IEEE Communications*, vol. 36, no. 7, pp. 58 – 67, July, 1998.

[139]. Straßer, M., Baumann, J., and Hohl, F., "Mole – A Java Based Mobile Agent System", *Proceedings of the ECOOP'96 workshop on Mobile Object Systems*, July 1996.

[140]. Stański, P., and Zaslavsky, A., "Expressing Dynamics of Mobile Agent Systems Using Ambient Calculus," *Proceedings. Of IEEE Computer Society*, pp. 434 – 439, 1998.

[141]. Stone, P., and Veloso, M., "Multiagent Systems: a Survey from a Machine Learning Perspective," *Autonomous Tobotics*, vol. 8, no. 3, July 2000.

[142]. Stoneburner, G., "Underlying Technical Models for Information Technology Security," NIST (National Institute of Standards and Technology), Special Publication 800-33, December 2001.

[143]. Stoneburner, G., Hayden, C., and Feringa, A., "Engineering Principles for Information Technology Security -- A Baseline for Achieving Security," NIST Special Publication 800-27, June 2001.

[144]. Swarup, V., "Trust Appraisal and Secure Routing of Mobile Agents," *DARPA Workshop on Foundations of Secure Mobile Code*, March 1997.

[145]. Taka, T., Mizuno, T., and Watanabe, T., "A Model of Mobile Agent Services Enhanced for Resource Restrictions and Security," *Proceedings of 1998 International Conference on Parallel and Distributed Systems (ICPADS '98)*.

[146]. Tan, H. K., and Moreau, L., "Extending Execution Tracing for Mobile Code Security," *Proceedings of Second International Workshop on Security of Mobile MultiAgent Systems (SEMAS'2002)*, pp. 51-59, 2002.

[147]. Tan, H. K., and Moreau, L., "Trust Relationships in a Mobile Agent System," *Mobile Agents*, LNCS, vol. 2240, pp. 15 – 30, 2001.

[148]. Tan, J. J., Titkov, L., and Neophytou, C., "Securing Multi-Agent Platform Communication," *Working Notes Second Int'l Workshop on Security of Mobile Multiagent Systems*, pp. 66 - 72, 2002.

[149]. Tardo, J., Valente, L., "Mobile Agent Security and Telescript," *Proceedings of IEEE COMPCON '96*, pp. 58 – 63, February 1996.

[150]. Thiagarajan, P. S., "Elementary Net Systems," *Petri Nets: Central Models and Their Properties*, Lecture Notes in Computer Science, no. 254, pp. 26 – 59, 1987.

[151]. Thirunavukkarasu, C., Finin, T., and Mayfield, J., "Secret Agents – a Security Architecture for the KQML Agent Communication Language," *Proceedings of 4th International Conference on Information and Knowledge Management - Workshop on Intelligent Information Agents*, Baltimore, Maryland, USA, Dec. 1995.

[152]. Thorn, T., "Programming Languages for Mobile Code," *ACM Computing Surveys*, vol. 29, no. 3, pp. 213 – 239, September 1997.

[153]. Tsai, J. J.P., and Ma, L., "Security Modeling and Analysis of Intelligent Mobile Systems," *Journal of Ubiquitous Computing and Intelligence*, 2006.

[154]. Tschudin, C., "Mobile Agent Security," *Intelligent Information Agents – Agent Base Information Discovery and Management on the Internet*, pp. 431 – 445, 1999.

[155]. Tveit, A., "A Survey of Agent-Oriented Software Engineering," *NTNU Computer Science Graduate Student Conference*, Norwegian University of Science and Technology, Trondheim, Norway, 2001.

[156]. Tygar, J. D., "Atomicity in Electronic Commerce," *Proceedings of the ACM Symposium on Principles of Distributed Computing*, May 1996.

[157]. Uhrmacher, A. M., Tyschler, P., and Tyschler, D., "Modeling Mobile Agents," *Proceedings of International Conference on Web-based Modeling & Simulation*, 1998.

[158]. Uhrmacher, A. M., Tyschler, P., and Tyschler, D., "Modeling and Simulation of Mobile Agents," *Future Generation Computer Systems*, vol. 17, no. 2, pp. 107 – 118, October 2000.

[159]. Uppuluri, P., and Sekar, R., Experiences with Specification-based Intrusion Detection, *Proceedings of Recent Advances in Intrusion Detection (RAID)*, October 2001.

[160]. Valk, R., "Petri Nets as Token Objects - An Introduction to Elementary Object Nets," *Proceedings of 19th International Conference on Application and Theory of Petri Nets (ICATPN'98)*, Lecture Notes in Computer Science, vol. 1420, pp. 1 – 25, 1998.

[161]. Valk, R., "Concurrency in Communicating Object Petri Nets," *Concurrent Object-Oriented Programming and Petri Nets, Advances in Petri Nets*, pp. 164 – 195, 2001.

[162]. Valk, R., "Relating Different Semantics for Object Petri Nets- Formal Proofs and Examples," *Technical Report FBI-HH-B-226*, pp. 1 – 50, University of Hamburg, Department for Computer Science, April 2000.

[163]. Valk, R., "On Processes of Object Petri Nets," *Technical Report FBI-HH-B-185/96*, pp. 1 – 45, University of Hamburg, Computer Science Department, 1996.

[164]. Van der Aalst, W. M. P., "Pi Calculus versus Petri Nets: Let us Eat Humble Pie Rather Than Further Inflate the Pi Hype," *http://tmitwww.tm.tue.nl/staff/wvdaalst/pi-hype.pdf*.

[165]. Verkoulen, P. A.C., "A Framework for Information Systems Design based on Object-Oriented Concepts and Petri Nets," *Proceedings of CAiSE Workshop on Formal Methods*, June 1994

[166]. Vigna, G., "Protecting Mobile Agents Through Tracing," *Proceedings of 3rd ECOOP Workshop on Mobile Object Systems*, 1997.

[167]. Vigna, G., "Cryptographic Traces for Mobile Agents," *Mobile Agents and Security*, Lecture Notes in Computer Science, vol.1419, pp. 137-153, 1998.

[168]. Vitek, J., and Castagna, G., "Towards a Calculus of Secure Mobile Computations," *Proceedings of Workshop on Internet Programming Languages*, Chicago, Illinois, 1998.

[169]. Vitek, J., and Castagna, G., "Seal: a Framework for Secure Mobile Computations," *Internet Programming Languages*, LNCS, vol. 1686, 1999.

[170]. Volpano D., and Geoffrey, S., "Language Issues in Mobile Program Security," *Proceedings of Mobile Agents and Security*, pp. 25 -43, 1998.

[171]. Walsh, T., Paciorek, N., and Wong, D., "Security and Reliability in Concordia," *Proceedings of the Thirty-First Annual Hawaii International Conference on System Sciences*, vol. VII, pp. 44 – 53, January 1998.

[172]. Wang, X., Hallstrom, J., and Baumgartner, G., "Reliability through Strong Mobility," *Proceedings of ECOOP workshop on Mobile Object Systems,* June, 2001.

[173]. Wermelinger, M., and Fiadeiro, J., "Connectors for Mobile Programs," *IEEE Transactions on Software Engineering* vol. 24, no. 1, pp. 331-341, January 1998.

[174]. White, J. E., "Telescript Technology: The Foundation for the Electronic Marketplace", *General Magic White Paper*, General Magic, Inc., 1994.

[175]. White, J. E., "Mobile Agents White Paper", General Magic, http://www.genmagic.com/technology/techwhitepaper.html, 1998.

[176]. Win, B. D., Bergh, J. V., Matthijs, F., Decker, B. D., and Joosen, W., "A Security Architecture for Electronic Commerce Applications," *Information Security for Global Information Infrastructures*, pp. 491-500, Kluwer Academic Publishers, 2000.

[177]. Wong, D., Pacoprek, N., Walsh, T., DiCelie, J., Young, M., and Peet, B., "Concordia: An Infrastructure for Collaborating Mobile Agents," *Proceedings of the First International Workshop on Mobile Agents (MA'97)*, vol. 1219 or Lecture Notes in Computer Science, pp. 86 – 97, 1997.

[178]. Xie, R., "Study on Modeling Mobile Objects in Distributed Computing Environment," *Proceedings of the 23rd Asian Conference on Remote Sensing*, 2002.

[179]. Xu, D., and Deng, Y., "Modeling Mobile Agent Systems with High Level Petri Nets," *Proceedings of IEEE International Conference on Systems, Man, and Cybernetics*, October 2000.

[180]. Xu, D, Yin, J., Deng, Y. and Ding, J., "A Formal Architectural Model for Logical Agent Mobility," *IEEE Transactions on Software Engineering*, vol. 29, no. 1, pp. 31 - 45, January 2003.

[181]. Xu, H. and Shatz, S. M., "A Framework for Model-Based Design of Agent-Oriented Software," *IEEE Transactions on Software Engineering*, vol. 29, no. 1, pp. 15 – 30, January 2003.

[182]. Yoo, M.-J., Merlat, W. and Briot, J.-P., "Modeling and Validation of Mobile Agents on the Web," *Proceedings of the International*

Conference on the Web-based Modeling & Simulation, vol. 30, no. 1, pp. 23 – 28, January 1998.

[183]. Zapf, M., Müller, H., and Geihs, k., "Security Requirements for Mobile Agents in Electronic Markets," *Trends in Distributed Systems for Electronic Commerce (TrEC '98)*, Hamburg, Germany, June 1998.

[184]. Zhang, Y., "An Authentication and Security Protocol for Mobile Computing," *Proceedings of IFIP World Conference on Mobile Communications*, pp.249-257, 1996.

[185]. Zhou, Y., Murata, T., and DeFanti, T. A., "Modeling and Performance Analysis Using Extended Fuzzy-Timing Petri Nets for Networked Virtual Environments," *IEEE Transactions on Systems, Man, and Cybernetics - PartB: Cybernetics*, vol. 30, no. 5, October 2000.

[186]. Zuberek, W. M., "Performance Study of Distributed Generation of State Spaces Using Colored Petri Nets," *Proceedings of the Fourth International Workshop on Practical Use of Coloured Petri Nets and the CPN Tools*, pp. 81 – 98, August 28-30, 2002.

[187]. NetCASE - a Petri Net based Method for Database Application Design and Generation, *Research Report 11-95*, University of Koblenz.

Index

ABEAS, 172
access control, 17, 38
Access Control Lists, 20, 130
access matrix, 129
Accountability, 7, 39
Action Security, 138
active migration, 95
Advanced Encryption Standard, 27
Agent Tcl, 41
Ajanta, 42
ambient, 56
anomaly detection, 23
Anonymity, 40
anti-virus software, 30
application-level gateway, 30
Ara, 43
Assurance, 7
asymmetric cryptography, 26
audit, 22
authentication, 16
Authentication, 7, 38
authorization, 38
Authorization, 8, 128
Authorization Policy, 131
authorization table, 21, 129
autonomous action, 96
autonomous occurrence, 63
Availability, 8, 39
bi-marking, 62, 75
blackbox, 54
Boundedness, 156
capabilities, 21
circuit-level, 29
code on demand, 2
Computing with Encrypted Functions, 54
Concurrency, 158
Confidentiality, 8, 38
critical tokens, 144

cryptographic tracing, 53
cryptography, 24
dangerous-party list, 87, 114
Data Encryption Standard, 27
Data Security, 136
data state, 1
Denial of Service, 11, 35, 36
Design/CPN, 143
differ-remove arc, 71
digital signature, 17, 52
discretionary access control, 19
driven transition, 73, 139
driving transition, 73, 139
Elementary Net System, 61
Elementary Object System, 61
environment net, 61
exclusively conditioned transitions, 101, 147
execution state, 1
Extended Elementary Object System, 73
extended interaction relation, 72
external place, 68, 75
external transition, 68
Fairness, 40
firewall, 28
home net, 68
identifier pair, 83
Integer Factorization Problem, 27
Integrity, 8
integrity checker, 32
interaction, 63
interaction relation, 63
internal place, 68, 75
internal transition, 68
intrusion detection, 22
Intrusion Detection Systems, 22
JAMES, 55
Java, 42

Jumping Beans, 44
mandatory access control, 18
Man-In-The-Middle, 13
Masquerade, 35
message authentication code, 17
misuse detection, 23
M-net, 138
mobile agent, 2, 1
mobile agent style token, 144
mobile agent system, 1
monitor, 31
mutual authentication, 125
Net within Net, 57
non-participation firing, 71
Non-repudiation, 9
Non-Repudiation, 39
object nets, 61
Object Oriented, 59
occurrence graph, 152
Odyssey, 45
OPN, 60
packet filtering, 28
padded cell, 50, 51
participation firing, 72
passive migration, 95
Petri Nets, 59
Privacy, 38
program, 1
Proof Carrying Code, 51
proxy server, 29
public key cryptography, 26
Reachability, 156
reachability graph, 152
reactive action, 96
registration table, 85
remote evaluation, 1

Remove Procedure Call, 1
remove-restore mechanism, 112
role-based access control, 19
RSA, 27
Safe TCL, 51
sandbox, 87
Sandbox, 50
scanner, 31
Seal Calculus, 56
SEAL Calculus, 54
shared-key cryptography, 25
single-key cryptography, 25
S-net, 138
specification based detection, 24
state appraisal, 53
state machine, 62
stateful multilayer inspection firewall,
    30
strong mobility, 1, 110
structural state machine, 62
symmetric key cryptography, 25
synchronous firing security mechanism,
    138
system net, 61
Telescript, 45
test arc, 69
token nets, 61
Token Pool, 66
transport, 63
Trust Server, 88
trusted-role-based policy, 132
unary Elementary Object System, 62
update arc, 70
Voyager, 46
weak mobility, 1, 110
Weak Mobility, 115